Believe *IT* to Receive *IT*

Activate the Miracles Waiting for You

BERNADETTE RODEBAUGH

BELIEVE IT TO RECEIVE IT

Design by Transcendent Publishing

ISBN: 978-1-0878-9473-7

Printed in the United States of America.

Dedication

For my best friend Duke, who is now in heaven. When I knew the time was getting closer for you to leave me and go to a better place, I asked you, "How much longer do we have together?" With profound intensity, you looked deep into my eyes and the message was clear: *Until you finish this book.* From that moment forward you and I began to take daily walks that provided me with much-needed breaks from my writing. During these walks, I also began to find and collect heart-shaped rocks. It was quite amazing at the time, and even more that to this day I still find these heart-shaped rocks everywhere I go. I know this is your way of telling me you are still with me, even though I cannot see you. You were definitely my best friend and earth angel, and now you are my angel in heaven watching over me. Thank you for your love and for keeping your unspoken promise to stay with me until this book was done.

If you would like to know what Bernadette does with these heart-shaped rocks, please visit BelieveItToReceiveIt.com

Contents

Introduction

We Will Never Talk About This Again

*D*o you feel lost, alone, possibly forsaken, forgotten, stuck or backed into a dark corner in some or all areas of your life? Are you rapidly losing hope that your situation will change or ever get better? Do you feel this way because society, your friends and/or family believe and agree that your situation is hopeless and that you have limited choices because of your education, financial status, family issues, health diagnosis or the history of who you have been in the past?

If so, you've come to the right place. Nobody should feel lost or alone in a world filled with billions of people, and nobody should feel like giving up, regardless of their current situation. Why? Because everyday *trillions* of miracles happen around the world to somebody, somewhere. WHY NOT YOU, NEXT?

Some of you may be wondering how I could make such a bold statement about not giving up despite the circumstances. Some of you may even be getting angry or defensive about it, and that's fine; it's just the space you're in right now. Helping to shift you out of that space is the purpose of this book. As for me, I can make this statement because I have been to the darkest places in my mind, body and soul—my own personal *hell on earth.*

During That Time in My Life I Had:

- An assortment of different physical conditions that were unbearable, life-threatening and, according to my doctors, incurable. Their advice: find a way to live with it or take more pills.
- Severe depression and anxiety that was crippling and created a life for me that was not really living.
- Considered leaving my newborn son with family because I believed he would have a better life without me in it.
- Been frozen in fear and despair, not knowing what to do next.
- Lived through many dark nights of the soul, literally, when I cried myself to sleep and/or woke up with fear and anxiety so severe my heart felt as if it would burst out of my chest.
- Screamed at God and asked why He had forsaken me.
- Looked into the eyes of my family members and asked for help or direction as to what I should do next, only to have them look back at me with fear and confirmation that my situation was hopeless.

I then MIRACULOUSLY found a SLIVER of LIGHT shining through the grey storm clouds blanketing my life. This sliver of light came in the form of HEALING TOOLS that revealed the answers I needed, at the exact right times I needed them, to guide me to "The Next Best Step" that would take me toward the miracles I was looking for (or, more accurately, that had been waiting for me). These tools began to heal me—first my soul, then my mind and then my body. They healed all areas of my life. I had only to BELIEVE IT to RECEIVE IT, the IT being "Inner Transformation."

Who I Was Before the Healing is Something I Do Not Talk About...

In fact, this will be the last time I discuss that period (the worst in my life!) with such detail. Why? Because of the many lessons I've learned in the twenty-two years since then, the most profound was that THOUGHTS BECOME THINGS. Here is an example: the two-year period in which I wrote this book was the first time I had really thought about my past issues since my Healing and Complete Transformation eighteen years earlier. Interestingly, during that time, one of my horrific health issues reappeared! This was the Universe verifying to me that indeed, thoughts do become things, and this is why I DO NOT talk about anything I DO NOT want to be true or a part of my current or future experience. Thankfully, by this time I knew what to do immediately to transform the situation. I was also more motivated than ever to share this information and help you reprogram the thoughts that are becoming unwanted "things" in your life, and to let you know that you too can be guided to YOUR NEXT BEST STEP to ACTIVATE the MIRACLES that have been waiting for you!

What follows is my own (past) personal hell and dramas. I share this to illustrate the transformation that is possible for you, as well as to help you to not feel so alone or that you are a lost cause. As you read this, keep in mind that each person's problems are different; most of mine were health issues that affected all other areas of my life. In other words, it was my Achilles' heel that kept reentering my world as I walked through my life, creating pain and suffering wherever I went. As you read through this book, beware of your own Achilles' heel and how it impacts your career, relationships, prosperity, self-worth, and so on. Don't worry, though, because the tools I share in this book can help transform all areas of your life too.

My Story

For the first twenty-five years of my life I had constant health problems; it was one thing after another and sometimes several things at once. Doctors regularly told me, "We don't know what's wrong with you"; "We don't know why you're not responding to the medicine"; or "Let's give you another pill and see if that one works." As time went on, I began to expect and accept that I would always have something wrong with my health, for example: a cold for every season; bouts of the flu that were worse than anyone else's; mysterious pain or severe stomach issues that disrupted my daily life, and so on. Generally feeling bad and being unhealthy was just a part of being me.

The years between the ages of twenty-five and twenty-eight were the darkest of my life. It began with an unexpected pregnancy, followed by an unexpected marriage and a move hours away from my hometown and my parents, all of which I was unprepared for mentally, physically and financially. Add a predisposition to expect the worst to the mix and, sure enough, the worst came knocking at my door.

Suddenly, in addition to my normal ailments, I had all-day morning sickness, deep depression, and anxiety so severe I didn't want to leave my house. Even after the shock of my pregnancy and my new life wore off, I could barely eat, I slept most of the day away and I was awake most of the night. The anxiety made me fearful of everything in my new environment. I even remember closing the curtains and the doors as tight as I could so I wouldn't be reminded that other people were out in the real world, happy and feeling good and going about the business of living. In truth, I was thinking, *How dare they go on with their lives when I feel like I'm dying inside—just an empty shell of a person with a black hole where my heart and soul used to live?* I share these raw emotions with you not only to be transparent about the space I was in, but so you can better understand depression and see that there is often no rhyme or reason to it. Things like getting pregnant and getting married can fill one person with joy while another is thrown into a downward spiral, whether it's because of their brain chemistry or the way their body reacts to the new stressors; still others might be triggered by past experiences and traumas. If you or someone you know is dealing with depression or anxiety, know that it is *not* your/their fault; one cannot just think it away!

What Major Depression Can Feel Like

When speaking to someone who has never experienced severe depression or anxiety, I ask them to imagine waking up one day to find themselves in a scene from *The Silence of the Lambs*. The movie, which stars Jodie Foster and Anthony Hopkins, is about a serial killer who throws his naked victims in a deep, dark, manmade dirt pit and slowly starves them. Well, depression feels like waking up in that deep dark cold pit, only instead of mud it is filled with dread. You have no idea how you got there or why; there is no light, so you can't see where you are or how to climb out. You also have no energy and your thoughts feel confused and foggy because you're so overwhelmed with helplessness. You continue to feel worse and worse as the extraordinarily long days turn into months and then years. This deep dark nightmare keeps you filled with fear and anxiety; your mind runs over and over on a loop of negative thoughts until you cannot imagine ever finding a way out.

I often have heard people say they don't understand why their loved one committed suicide, or ask what kind of person could leave their baby at a fire department. Unfortunately, I understand all too well. It's because they already feel dead inside, and they honestly don't know what else to do. Oftentimes, neither do their doctors. I lived with severe depression for almost three years and though my doctors were using all their resources nothing relieved it completely. It wasn't until I started using the tools I teach in this book, in conjunction with medical help, that my life began to change.

What I Learned

My struggle with deep depression taught me not to judge homeless people who stand on the street corner begging for money or food; I no longer wonder why they don't just get a job or get off the drugs and alcohol. I now understand that people don't end up homeless if they are mentally, physically and spiritually healthy, and I know without a doubt that I could have been homeless too or would have had to leave my son at a fire department door, because even in the depths of my darkness I knew he deserved more than I could provide for him.

Fortunately, I had the support of two aunts who lived close by. They offered me tireless love and support, especially when I was struggling as a new mother (which was often!). My husband was also an angel, working twelve to eighteen hours a day to support our family when I was too depressed to get out of bed, leave the house, or even think about holding down a job.

When my son was three months old, I finally received the psychiatric help I needed. By that time, I had lost faith and hope of ever coming out of the depression and anxiety alive, let alone being able to have a healthy, happy and normal life. Thankfully, I still had the presence of mind to reach out and call my obstetrician. When I told him I couldn't stop crying, he recommended I *immediately* start seeing a psychiatrist who specialized in depression. This was not what I wanted to hear, but it was what I *needed* to hear.

Admitting I needed help was the hardest thing I had ever done, but it provided the first glimmer of hope that there was a way out of the dark pit of hell that was slowly killing me.

Admitting I needed medication to function at my best wasn't easy either; nor is it what people expect to hear from a teacher and mentor who speaks about believing in miracles. And that is precisely why I'm telling my story, because I now know and believe that your answers will only show up in the medium you BELIEVE they can show up in. My answer came in the form of medicine because that was the miracle I expected and asked for. When you use the tools in this book you can ask for your miracle to show up any way you want; remember, though, that your belief must be aligned with this desire. At the same time, be grateful for whatever way your miracle and/or solution shows up, because it's most likely exactly what you need, even if at first it doesn't look like it.

This is exactly what happened in my case. As much as I hated the thought of taking medicine to help me out of my depression, once it began to work, I realized that I had not felt this "kind of good" since before I hit puberty. I learned that for most of my life, I had not been producing enough serotonin and other chemicals in the brain that help people adjust to different types of stress. Change, even good change, is stressful, so it's no wonder that when I experienced a complete, unplanned life makeover I went down into a black hole fast.

The relief I felt when my depression and anxiety lifted is indescribable; however, it wasn't long before my Achilles' heel showed up again, this time in the form of new health challenges. At that time, I had only learned half the tools I teach in this book, and I didn't yet understand how to use them to prevent illness and other life dramas.

I suddenly began breaking out in severe, unexplained hives. Each day, they took over my body, moving anywhere from head to toes, and I never knew if and when they might cause my throat to close up and block my airway. I lived in constant fear that I would have to use an EpiPen in public or when I was home alone with my now two-year-old son.

To make matters worse, my husband and I were on the verge of losing our house—an exhausting and frightening situation that seemed to go on forever. However, once I started applying ALL the tools from this book to the health and financial areas of my life these challenges came to a quick and miraculous resolution.

You Too Can Turn Lemons into Lemonade, With No Need for Vodka!

The information I share with you in this book saved my life on many levels. It not only helped me heal my physical issues, it also helped our family heal financially. It is the reason we never became homeless.

How did this happen? These tools guided me and my husband to the right people, places and things we needed at just the right time, *even though my husband wasn't aware of it at the time.* This is a key point of what I am teaching here: my husband did not actively participate in using these tools, and *still they worked for both of us.* My husband is not the kind of person who believes in miracles or prays or talks of spirituality or God; in fact, if you were to ask him today how we overcame that desperate time in our life, I'm sure he would say it was "hard work," "luck" or his own ideas. I, however, know these "ideas" were actually divine Inner Guidance and synchronistic thoughts that led to events that answered our prayers or provided miraculous solutions to our situation. It doesn't matter what you call sparks of inspiration; all that matters is that you take action AND DON'T QUESTION IT. While I wholeheartedly agree that his physical efforts (i.e. going to work every day) contributed profoundly to our changed circumstances, I KNOW that there was more to it than that. It was what I was doing *behind the scenes.* This is what I teach here— how to use your Inner Guidance to find or call in the answers you are seeking. This will serve as the tipping point, as your Higher Power works through other people, places and things on your behalf, especially when you have limited abilities or resources, as was the case with me and my health issues.

This book will provide you with easy and doable activation steps to help you believe (or at the very least, hope) that there is a way out of your darkness, even though you cannot see the light at the end of the tunnel... yet!

It DOES NOT MATTER if the miracles you are seeking:

- Are needed solutions, answered prayers, hope or guidance, et cetera.
- Are for you or people you love or even people you don't care about.
- Are for people who BELIEVE or DO NOT BELIEVE in miracles, God/Higher Power or Universal energy.

It only takes a sliver of belief and hope to begin the process of activating your miracles!

Things to Keep in Mind as We Proceed:

Throughout this book I use the words "Higher Power" to explain the unforeseen forces that these tools activate. I do this because I want to be able to reach as many people as possible, including and especially those who (like I was at one point) are losing faith, and those who (like my husband) want to BELIEVE to RECEIVE more miracles in their life but for whom the words "God," "faith" or "miracles" are not comprehensible...*yet!* Please substitute Higher Power with whatever word you feel most comfortable with: God, The Universe, Universal Energy, Angels, Guides, Jehovah, Father, Higher Self, et cetera.

> **PLEASE NOTE:**
>
> *This book is not meant to take the place of doctors, medication or medical treatment. Please continue to work with your healthcare practitioners and prescribed medications. However, the information in this book will positively enhance any self-care and/or medical care you are receiving and can contribute to your miraculous results.*

Shall we begin now to activate your miracles?

Chapter 1

The Intrusive Message

*I*n the beginning, the message began to reveal itself as I tried to fall asleep. It came in the form of a sentence repeating in my head over and over again like a broken record: *In the deep depths of your soul you have a secret…In the deep depths of your soul you have a secret… In the deep depths of your soul you have a secret…*

Even though I heard this sentence in my own voice, I still wondered where it was coming from. Oddly enough, it never crossed my mind that I might be going crazy; instead, I had an internal knowingness that without a doubt this information was important and I should write it down—immediately!—because one day I would share it with others. This did not make sense to me at the time—I didn't understand why this sentence was so important or when or why I should share it. I just knew that if I wrote it down, the sentence would stop repeating itself… for now.

But I didn't write it down. Each time it happened I told myself that I would do it when I awoke (though I knew I wouldn't) and instead tried to block the repeated humming words that worked like a lullaby in reverse, because unlike other lullabies this one was meant to keep me awake. Since I would eventually fall asleep without writing it down, I soon began to hear my lullaby during the day, like when I was taking a shower, cleaning, or driving—basically any time I was on autopilot and didn't have to concentrate on what I was doing. This annoying, persistent sentence would consistently repeat itself and I would keep ignoring it. This went on for about a year, until one day, for no apparent reason at all, I surprised myself and finally wrote it down. Suddenly, magically, the rest of the message revealed itself to me:

In the deep depths of your soul you have a secret. Do you wish to find it, or be left in the dark? Turn the page now, if you are ready to start the journey of the message from your soul.

As I wrote the complete message in my journal, I was both amazed and puzzled. This information felt like it had come from me and yet from somewhere else, almost like a "download" into my brain but in my own voice!

I then put the journal away and the lullaby stopped—I NEVER HEARD IT AGAIN!

The year was 1997 and I was twenty-four years old. Almost immediately after that I found out I was pregnant, which began the downward spiral I mentioned earlier and ultimately led me to ask for Inner Guidance and the tools I needed to get me out of darkness.

I have often wondered whether I would have avoided some of that darkness had I asked for that guidance earlier. The truth is, I never thought of it again or understood the importance of the mysterious message until eighteen years later when I accidentally came across that old journal. I was then forty-one and recently retired from a twenty-four-year career as a hairstylist. Most people might think it was an odd time to walk away—I had more clients than I could handle and was making more money than ever before. I was in a place every hairstylist dreams of. But for some reason, the busier I got the more miserable I became! This was a mystery to me, because for a long time I had been very happy with my career and then, almost overnight, I just wasn't. Nothing had changed externally, but I had changed on some deep level that was unexplainable. This drastic shift in my feelings told me that my Inner Guidance was speaking to me. I was being told that it was time to move on, because there was something important for me to do and it was waiting for me.

That's when I decided to retire and use my Inner Guidance to transform my career life. How was I going to do this? I had no idea! As I waited for my Inner Guidance to tell me MY NEXT BEST STEP, I began doing my favorite thing to do when I need an answer: I detoxed my house (I talk more about this in Chapter 7). It was during this clearing that I ran across the old journal, and as soon as I read that sentence it was like a switch—the same one that had been turned off since I wrote the entry eighteen years earlier—had suddenly been flipped on. Suddenly, pictures began flashing through my mind—pictures of me doing workshops in the future, writing this book and teaching others these tools I had been learning and using during those eighteen years to transform my life. The guidance I'd been asking for had arrived!

Plug into Your Miracles TOOL

Have you ever started your day and you just didn't feel "on," like maybe one of the electrical switches in your brain forgot to get started with the rest of you? I call this not being "plugged in" to your HIGHER SOURCE OF ENERGY, which is your HIGHER POWER and INNER GUIDANCE. The good news is that you can get plugged in again whenever you want. The technique I am about to share involves a *conscious reconnection* to your Source Energy through the visualization of you ASKING for and RECEIVING guidance outside of your human self and accepted limitations. It is actually very similar to prayer or visualization meditation.

I suggest that you plug into your Higher Source of Energy every morning because this starts your day off with positive expectations. The easiest way is to incorporate it into your regular routine, for example, while in the shower, which is a morning habit for many and, as I explain below, can become a very powerful aspect of this visualization. If you forget, as I sometimes do, to do it in the shower, just plug in whenever you remember. You can even do it while driving in the car, as long as you keep your eyes open!

You can also use this tool when you are having a stressful day or feeling really tired and exhausted, *because any time you're tired, irritable, feeling lost or depressed it's a sign that you have lost your inner connection to your Higher Power.* The time and place do not matter; the key is to consciously EXPECT TO RECEIVE the ANSWERS that will guide you to YOUR NEXT BEST STEP to the MIRACLES you have been asking for!

The "Plugging into Miracles" Visualization Tool

1. Say, "Please surround me now, _____." (Fill in your word of choice—i.e. Higher Power, God, Universe, et cetera.)

2. Say, "I ask you to help me BELIEVE and RECEIVE your CRYSTAL-CLEAR GUIDANCE in all areas of my life, especially the following: _____." (Include any area of your life that you are worried about, lost or needing help with.)

3. Say, "Thank You, Thank You, Thank You." *REPEAT THIS STEP THREE TIMES, OUT LOUD.*

4. Close your eyes and imagine your Higher Source is now surrounding and protecting you with a bright white light that has sparkling diamond essence and the properties of healing, Crystal-Clear Guidance and unconditional love.

5. Take a deep breath through your nose, and imagine that you can feel this diamond light healing all areas of your mind, body and soul. Then blow out through your nose, releasing and clearing out any worries and concerns. If you're in the shower, imagine this is old energy going down the drain, rinsing off you easily and effortlessly, or into the ground wherever you currently are sitting or standing. This old energy is now recycled into positive energy through Mother Earth.

6. Imagine sending gratitude to Mother Earth for transforming this energy.

7. Take three more deep breaths while you imagine this cleansing light. Do this until you are RELAXED and AT EASE.

8. Now put both your hands on your heart space. Imagine that inside this area you can see and feel the same beautiful white light, about the size of a light bulb, with your own unique essence. This is your inner guiding light and internal compass.

9. Take three more deep breaths, and with each exhale expand your inner light out. As it connects with your Higher Power,

it becomes an aura of light, fanning out from you in every direction, as if you are the center of the sun. Imagine this light expanding out through you, all the way to the heavens and down through the center of Mother Earth.

10. Now say out loud, "Thank you, my Divine Light, for connecting with my Higher Power energy, so that I now have crystal-clear guidance and protection throughout my day, wherever I go, whomever I'm with, and whatever I do. My day is now filled with miracles for my highest possibilities in every area of my life! Thank You, Thank You, Thank You!"

Now that you're connected to your inner source of guidance and protection, you can count on it at any time through the day. Use this tool every morning to strengthen your awareness, because the more you use your inner guidance the stronger it becomes. You will never doubt it again!

Miracle Guidance TOOL

Our Higher Power (or God, The Universe, et cetera) is always communicating with us. In fact, today, this hour or even possibly this moment you are receiving guidance toward YOUR NEXT BEST STEP that will lead you toward your miracle! The problem is we were never taught how to read this special language, so we doubt the information that comes to us or discredit the signs that are guiding us. Maybe we think it doesn't seem logical or that it seems too good to be true; we wonder, *how could the answer I'm looking for possibly be this simple?* We spend so much time trying to debunk the guidance that oftentimes when we finally decide to follow it the moment or opportunity has already passed. If this happens, don't worry; when you are receiving answers from your Higher Power the guidance or opportunity keeps reappearing until you take that step that you're being guided to. This tool is one of my favorites and easiest to understand when it comes to helping us to become more confident with this Inner Guidance.

You are *Already* Receiving Inner Guidance as a *Seer* or *Feeler* or *Both*:

There are countless ways in which our Higher Power and Inner Guidance communicates with us, which can feel challenging or confusing when we are stressed and need a definitive answer *now*. That's where this wonderfully simple tool comes in. I often use it with my clients and have found it to be the easiest to learn, remember and use during urgent times, because it focuses only on what you FEEL and/or what you SEE. It will help you figure out YOUR NEXT BEST STEP.

How to Use:

Think of a particular situation or dilemma you are facing and two different choices you have to deal with it. Imagine holding one of the choices in your left hand and the other in your right hand and ask yourself:

Does one of the choices FEEL lighter or heavier than the other? Does one choice seem to FEEL good or bad, relative to the other?

Or

When you imagine these two choices, does one LOOK or SEEM lighter or brighter than the other; does one seem darker or duller?

Or

Can you easily imagine your future if you were to move forward with one choice as opposed to the other? Another way to do this is by asking yourself where each choice will take you.

If this seems difficult in the beginning, write down the two choices on separate pieces of paper and hold one in each hand. You may find that one of the papers looks lighter or brighter, or dull and cloudy; it may feel heavy, dirty, or unappealing.

NOTE:

Don't worry if you cannot immediately get the message, for it can come through subtly. Also, most people have one Inner Guidance ability that is stronger than the other (i.e. one person's primary source of information comes from their feelings, while another's comes from seeing). The more you use it, the more crystal-clear your Guidance will become; the more you will trust this Guidance, the more you will begin to receive it through both SEEING and FEELING!

You Can Use This Tool for *Everything!* Here are a few of my favorite examples:

- **Driving:** When I'm running late and stopped at a light, I will ask my Inner Guidance which direction I should take in order to arrive on time (one direction will seem illuminated and feel better to me than the other).

- **Gambling:** When playing roulette, I use it to choose between red and black, or to choose the numbers (certain numbers will be more appealing to me than others and feel better when I look at them). I also use it to pick a slot machine (in a section of machines, one will almost "glow," as if it's calling my name). *Side note: Since using this tool I have never come home with less money than I went gambling with.*

- **Multiple-choice questions on an exam:** I used this often when I was in college and hadn't studied for an exam or just simply couldn't decide which answer was correct. (One choice would look bolder and feel better to me than the others.)

- **Choosing between two cars to buy:** My husband says I'm the only person he knows who can sit in a car and, without even test driving it, know whether or not I want to buy it. (I will feel like one of the cars is already mine or I will feel "at home" in it. Sometimes I will also see a picture of my family in the car at some point in the future.)

- **A friend wants a second opinion (between two choices) when making a decision:** I often get a "good" feeling (i.e. goose bumps or the hair will rise on my body or head) about the choice I feel guided to suggest to her.

- **Choosing between two jobs I've been offered:** While in the waiting room before the interview, I will already feel "at home" or that I can easily see myself working there in the future, or I immediately know this is not the job for me.

Be Conscious

Once you get in touch with your Seeing and Feeling Inner Guidance, start to pay attention to your thoughts while doing miscellaneous activities that allow you to go on autopilot (i.e. as you're drifting off to sleep at night, driving, taking a shower, cleaning or exercising), as this is when you're likely to have reoccurring thoughts or get seemingly "random" ideas. Remember, this is how I began to hear my Inner Guidance, and I often wonder what would've been different in my life if I had acknowledged it back then and understood I could ask what is, "MY NEXT BEST STEP?"

WEEK ONE ACTIVATION STEP: CHOOSING YOUR "NEXT BEST STEP"

Each Miracle Activation requires you to take the TOOLS learned in each chapter and incorporate them into your life through ACTION STEPS; this begins the Miracle Activation process. This first Action Step is easy: you simply CALL upon your Higher Power of choice, then ASK for crystal-clear guidance about some issue or area of your life. Let's try it, using this book as an example.

After calling on your Higher Power, ask, "What is the NEXT BEST STEP for me with regard to the information in this book?" Ask silently or out loud as you look at the following choices:

1. "Should I turn the page NOW to start the *Believe IT to Receive IT* journey to create my miraculous ideal Life?" *Now, imagine turning this page. Is the next page bright and light, as if it holds the answers you have been looking for? Or does it seem dark or difficult or heavy to turn the page?*

2. "Should I close this book now, admit to myself that it's not the ideal time for me to learn the *Believe IT to Receive IT* tools, and instead save it for a later date?" *Imagine yourself putting this book on a table or bookshelf for later. Does this option feel like a relief? Or, do you see yourself picking it right back up?*

3. "Should I admit this book is not for me and pass it on to the next person I talk to who seems ready for an Inner Transformation?" *Imagine giving this book to another person. Is this image crystal-clear and easy to see? Or does it feel wrong or uncomfortable? (If you are guided to give this book away, thank you for sharing it! Please accept my blessings, wherever your journey takes you!)*

Congratulations on turning the page and choosing to begin your *Believe IT to Receive IT* journey! Here are some helpful hints to keep you aligned with your MIRACLES while using this book:

At the end of each chapter you'll find two Positive Affirming Mantras and/or visualizations designed to be RIPPED OUT or CUT IN HALF and HUNG UP.

- Place these mantras in different areas in your home, car, work, or anywhere you want and need positive reminders. The idea here is to REPEATEDLY SEE them (consciously and unconsciously), which will help ACTIVATE and REPROGRAM your thinking and ACCELERATE your MIRACLES.
- This repeating of new positive thoughts will eventually delete the old negative thoughts. Because consistently SEEING and SAYING what you want to be TRUE helps ATTRACT and CREATE the life you want on a conscious and unconscious level.

I Now Receive
Crystal-Clear
Guidance
To
My Next Best Step,
To My
Miraculous Life.

✂

PLUGGING INTO MIRACLES SUMMARY

Hang up to read while getting ready.

1. Say out loud: "Please surround me now, (insert your Higher Power word). I ask you to help me to BELIEVE and RECEIVE your CRYSTAL-CLEAR GUIDANCE in all areas of my life, especially in the following areas:_____."

2. Close your eyes and imagine Your Higher Power surrounding you with a protective light with a diamond essence and qualities of healing, crystal-clear guidance and unconditional love.

   - Inhale deeply through your nose and imagine that you can feel this light healing all areas of your mind, body and soul. Exhale through your mouth while releasing any worries and concerns.

   - Take three more deep breaths and continue visualizing until you feel relaxed and RELAXED and at EASE.

   - Put both your hands on your heart space and imagine that you can see and feel the same beautiful light inside you.

   - Take three more deep breaths and with each exhalation expand your inner light out. As it connects with your Higher Power, it becomes an aura of light, fanning out from you in every direction, as if you are the center of the sun. Imagine this light expanding out through you, all the way to the heavens and down through the center of Mother Earth.

   - Say out loud: "Thank you my Divine light for connecting with my Higher Power energy so that I NOW have crystal-clear guidance and protection throughout my day—wherever I go and whatever I do. My day is now filled with miracles for my highest possibilities in every area of my life! Thank You, Thank You, Thank You!"

Chapter 2

Intensify Believing to Receive, ASAP!

*I*n the last chapter you learned how to call upon your Higher Power and ask for guidance. If you are reading this, it means you were guided to turn the page and continue with this book, which I BELIEVE means you are ready to RECEIVE the Inner Transformation you are wanting and needing so you can be guided to YOUR NEXT BEST STEP toward the miracles you are seeking. In this chapter I'm going to share with you how to speed up the process. Don't forget to continue to PLUG IN and ask for Inner Guidance each day and throughout this guidebook.

How to Accelerate Believing

Have you ever had another person believe in you or your ability more than you believed in yourself? And, as a result of their belief in you, did you begin to believe in yourself and your ability too? If so, you are very blessed! This is a powerful (and often missing) ingredient that acts as an accelerant, bringing your desired miracles to you even faster.

When This Hit Home for Me

I learned this powerful tool in 2008, during another very challenging time for my family. Three years earlier, I had retired from hairdressing for the first time because I was feeling burnt out and hoping to find a new career that had more meaning for my life and soul. I also wanted to stay home with our son, then five years old, and was fortunate that my husband's construction business was doing so well that I had the freedom to do so. During that time, I did consider my next career path but I hadn't found anything I felt aligned with. I was also still in the process of learning more of the tools I would later use in this book.

Like so many others, our financial circumstances were affected by the Great Recession, and we now had to find a way to bring more money in. I began looking for work but couldn't find anything. Then my husband, who was just thirty-three years old, had a heart attack. In an instant, our situation went from nerve-wracking to terrifying. After the attack he was unable to work for six weeks, during which I was still unable to find a job.

We were desperate, and though working as a hairstylist again was the last thing I wanted to do, I didn't appear to have much choice. I wasn't getting hired for any of the other jobs I applied for, and besides, they were only paying eight to ten dollars an hour—not enough to sustain us.

During this time my dad often came over to visit and check in on us, to see how we were doing. I had confided to him that I was afraid we would lose our dream house, which my husband had built for us with his own hands. Dad told me about a woman he'd heard about from my aunt; the woman, a manicurist, owned a little salon in a house. Maybe, he suggested, I could rent a room from her and do hair? At first, I dismissed the idea, just as I had when my aunt told me about the very same opportunity. I would have to pay her rent, I said, and how would I do that with no clientele? What I really needed was a place where I had a guaranteed weekly salary, even if it was only eight dollars an hour, or whatever the current minimum wage was.

"Bernadette, that's just crazy talk," Dad said, "because you need more money than those type of jobs are paying."

"I just don't think I can do hair anymore," I replied, "I've forgotten how to be a hairstylist! And of all the options I would have as a hairstylist, working at that woman's salon is the worst possible choice, because I would essentially be working alone. I haven't done hair for three years and would need other hairstylists to bounce ideas off of when I had a complex situation with color or other chemicals. *I just don't believe in myself or my abilities as a hairstylist anymore! And I don't have money to pay rent or the thousand dollars I'd need to buy my supplies!*"

I'll never forget what my dad said to me next: "Bernadette, I believe in you and I will loan you money to get started."

I wish I could say that I changed my mind instantly, but I didn't; in fact, I might've said something about him "not understanding the salon industry."

Dad let the subject drop that day, but over the next two weeks he continued to bring it up, saying I could make it work long enough to help take the stress off my husband while he got on his feet again. He was always gentle and encouraging, never forceful, and always emphasized that he believed in me. Each time he spoke of it I would think to myself how naïve he was about the salon business. In the meantime, I was desperately applying for any job that could guarantee me a weekly paycheck.

Then, in one day, two friends asked me to do their hair at my house, for which I made a hundred dollars. I remember looking down at all that money in my hands and feeling like I had won the lottery! Instantly, I saw myself going to that woman's little salon and renting the room. I then followed my Inner Guidance, even though I thought it was a ridiculous idea, since I would be paying money to work there instead of the other way around!

It felt even more ridiculous when I went to see the room. As the owner unlocked the door, she told me to ignore the mess; she was having a garage sale that weekend and was keeping all her stuff in the room until then. I wouldn't even be able to walk around. She then pushed open the door and turned on the light. *Instantly, I was in love and could see myself working there! It didn't matter that I couldn't walk into the salon—I honestly felt like I was home and I knew without a doubt that this was the answer to my prayers!* Sure enough, from the moment I began working at that salon unbelievable things began to happen for me. Not only did my dad invest in me and my business, but my aunt did as well.

This salon proved to be a once-in-a-lifetime opportunity with amazing little miracles that allowed me to instantly build my business, instead of having to wait years as is typical in the industry. Eventually my husband's business recovered and began to flourish as well. He was guided to go to North Dakota, where it was busier, which meant he was out of town for long periods of time. Fortunately, I was self-employed and could therefore adjust my schedule to be home for my son.

Now, when I look back at that time, I am amazed at how close I came to settling for a job that appeared to be the logical choice but in reality would not have allowed me to contribute to the household finances in a meaningful way. And no doubt I would have settled, if not for my dad's gentle encouragement and the prayers of my mother and aunts that I would find the "Divine ideal job" to help my family survive the recession and my husband's heart attack (I found out about these prayers later, after I had already started at the salon). *This is proof of the power of their BELIEF that I would find a MIRACLE JOB, even during a time when I was skeptical and didn't believe in myself and my abilities.*

For the next few years, I was a hairstylist again and *I was loving it!* In fact, I couldn't even remember why I had been so burned out three years earlier. My time at that little salon would also be my most prosperous up to that point. Most importantly, I learned a very valuable lesson: I could start with nothing—no clients, no money, no confidence in myself or my skills and NO interest in what I was being guided to do—and still end up where I wanted to be! The only requirement is that I follow what my Inner Guidance was telling me to do.

Create Your Own Miracle Team TOOL

Imagine how it would feel to have a team that believes in you and your desired miracle, no matter how hopeless your current situation seems and regardless of your education, financial status, birth inheritance, health diagnosis, or who you have been in the past.

This kind of TEAM AGREEMENT and likeminded support creates a powerful BELIEF in your own goals and in one another, which allows the MIRACULOUS ANSWERS you are seeking to come to you easier and seemingly effortlessly through your Inner Guidance, which is now INTENSIFIED BY TWO OR MORE PEOPLE WORKING TOGETHER and BELIEVING IN ONE ANOTHER AND THEIR UNLIMITED POSSIBILITIES!

Think of this team as sort of a book club, but unlike other book clubs it is designed to help you work with others who are also aligned and in agreement with doing the steps needed to TRANSFORM their lives. This TEAM AGREEMENT helps you stay motivated and accountable so that you do not self-sabotage or undermine your Inner Guidance as the miraculous NEXT STEPS and ANSWERS you are looking for start revealing themselves to you at RECORD SPEED! Since each member is now plugging in regularly to their own Inner Guidance, this automatically helps all members confirm the information that is coming to them, rather than second-guessing it.

This kind of agreement and feedback is profound and priceless as you and your teammates are guided individually and collectively to YOUR NEXT BEST STEP through each ACT-IVATION as it is put into motion by your physical ACTION STEPS in each chapter.

If you do not yet have a team, don't worry. Below I share four easy ACTION STEPS to help you create one. **I highly suggest that you and your team spend one week on each**

chapter to allow time to complete each ACTIVATION and its ACTION STEPS. This will enable you to successively incorporate each tool into your life without feeling rushed, and by the time you are done reading this book you will already be experiencing miracles in your life.

WEEK TWO ACTIVATION STEPS: CREATING YOUR "MIRACLE TEAM"

This week's action step is about creating a TEAM OF BELIEVERS who agree to believe in one another and their ability to TRANSFORM their lives REGARDLESS OF THEIR CURRENT REALITY. With this book's guidance, you and your team members will believe into reality whatever each of you is looking for (i.e. end results, goals, solutions, miracles, healing, answered prayers, et cetera). It is your BELIEF that creates the INNER TRANSFORMATION that ALLOWS the unbelievable outcomes you are wanting to find you!

First ACTION STEP: Activate Your Ideal Team

Begin by PLUGGING IN. Remember, any time you want to create something of importance it is always best to consciously get realigned with your Inner Guidance. During this time ask for your Miracle Club team members to easily and (seemingly) effortlessly be guided to you. Choose the date you want this to be accomplished by, including the month, day and year (I suggest you choose a date at least seven days from when you make the request).

Second ACTION STEP: "Who Do You Know?"

Answer the questions below without making judgments about who you think may be potential candidates for your team. The idea here is to get your juices flowing and ready for Divine inspiration and intervention.

Make a list of people you know personally (i.e. friends, family members, coworkers, et cetera).

_____

_____

_____

_____

_____

_____

_____

List ALL people you may NOT know personally but come to mind when you think of clubs or organizations you are connected to (i.e. church, sports teams, hobbies, clubs, networking groups, et cetera).

_____

_____

_____

_____

_____

_____

_____

List ALL your social media sites, personal and group accounts (i.e. Facebook, Twitter, Instagram, et cetera).

_____

_____

_____

_____

_____

_____

_____

Third ACTION STEP: Use Your Inner Guidance

When your list for potential Miracle Club team members feels complete, print or tear it out and hold it in your hand. Ask your Inner Guidance, "Which of these people or groups should I consider first as potential members?" Then, using the SEEING or FEELING exercise discussed in the previous chapter, begin to circle any names or places that stand out to you. They may seem bolder or brighter when you look at them, or you may feel good, happy or a knowingness about a particular name or that a particular place contains a future team member. Circle at least five choices from each group.

Fourth ACTION STEP: Reaching Out Then Release And Trust

Call, text or post on social media sites, using something similar to the following:

> **I'm creating a book club that helps you activate more MIRACLES in your life. This process is ACCELER-ATED with two or more people. If you are also wanting MORE MIRACLES IN YOUR LIFE, please contact me at_____. This book club is FREE; you need only acquire the book we are using, *Believe IT to Receive IT: Activate the Miracles Waiting for You,* by Bernadette Rodebaugh. It can be found on Amazon and at Barnes & Noble.**

Finally, take one last look at the list of potential team members and release it to The Universe and your Higher Power, knowing that the ideal members will be guided to you easily and effortlessly. Show faith or trust in this process by burning the list, tearing it up, flushing it down the toilet or putting it in the trash.

BELIEVE that this ACTIVATION STEP is now DONE!

BELIEF is the MAGNET that attracts your dreams into reality!

Guidelines for Your Book Club/Miracle Team

- This group should consist of at least two people (meaning you and at least one other) and no more than four people. This way, in a suggested one-hour team meeting everyone has at least ten minutes to talk with five minutes of input from other members.
- Be careful who you choose for your team. Don't assume that they'll be your closest friends and family. Sometimes those closest to you only remember your past experiences, mistakes, or doctor's diagnoses. They may not understand your NEW ABILITY to release the past and its previous hold on you and to be a CATALYST for creating a new miraculous future.
- All members need to read this book together so they understand the power and purpose of the team's weekly ACTION STEPS and their individual contributions.
- All members must agree to create a vision of the new aspects in their life that they want to improve. This means Dream Big, Bold and Unapologetically because nothing you can think of or dream about is TOO MUCH! (In the next chapter you will start putting these ideas on paper.)
- All members must be willing to do ALL the ACTION STEPS in this book.

Meeting Suggestions

- Schedule team meeting dates and times or meet weekly for the seven remaining weeks of this guidebook. Consider the use of conference calls via Skype, Zoom, or FaceTime, or apps such as Marco Polo and Voxer. Be open-minded about how to make this work.

- Share with one another in great detail what your vision of your "Transformed Life" feels and looks like. (Chapter 3 will go deeper into how you can create and share your IDEAL LIFE VISION with one another.)

- During weekly meetings spend at least five to fifteen minutes per team member reviewing how each is incorporating that chapter's ACTION STEPS into their daily routine and any challenges that may be arising while creating and believing in their IDEAL LIFE. **(Choose one member to set a timer so everybody has equal amounts of sharing time and nobody dominates the meeting.)**

- Each member must be conscientious and share when he/she receives Inner Guidance for the others (Use the tools from Chapter 1: "How are you receiving Divine Guidance?"). You will soon notice that your Inner Guidance is becoming more consistent and intense, now that you have committed to use it for a higher purpose, namely, the miraculous transformation of your own life and the lives of your team members. You will see that there really is POWER in two or more people joining together for an agreed-upon purpose!

- <u>Only during the first meeting should you discuss the negative life issues you are working on overcoming.</u> This is done solely for the purpose of educating the other members as to where you have been and where you want to go. **Make sure this part of the meeting is short and to the point, because talking about it and thinking**

about it will only create more of it. From this moment forward, THINK AND TALK ONLY ABOUT WHAT YOU WANT TO BE TRUE IN YOUR LIFE! Remind and help one another with this as you reword statements and phrases to a positive present tense when needed. (We will talk more about this in Chapter 3.)

Team of One

If you're unable find others to create a book club/team, don't stress! You can join our open *"Believe IT to Receive IT"* page on Facebook, which will provide you with a safe space and a likeminded tribe with whom to share your experiences.

I only *Think* and

Talk about what

I WANT TO BE

True

From this moment

Forward!

✂

My IDEAL *Life*

and

My IDEAL *Team*

is

Now EASILY

Revealed

to Me!

✂

Chapter 3

Your Super Power

*T*hroughout this book you will learn different techniques that help you BELIEVE without a shadow of a doubt that whatever you want is possible, because once you BELIEVE in the POSSIBILITY of the UNBELIEVABLE becoming TRUE, that's when the magic and miracles begin to happen! This process begins with something I like to call the "Domino Effect" because of its innate ability to create positive shifts in your beliefs, which are needed to create a chain reaction for your Inner Transformation to take place. Remember, it's the little steps you take in life that get you to where you want to be!

That said, transformation does not only come with baby steps. Sometimes, it is dramatic and immediate. Later in this chapter I will also share with you my favorite example of how we can, by virtue of our thoughts, INSTANTLY change our physical bodies. This knowledge, which has been backed up by science, had a profound impact on me and my life. I began to understand the POWER OF BELIEVING, which jumpstarted my journey of healing in all areas of my life. Any time you feel like you're losing hope and don't know what to do next in your life, come back to this chapter to remember that the unbelievable becoming BELIEVABLE is ONLY A BELIEF AWAY!

Transformational ABCs

I have found that the best transformational tools are also the simplest. That's why I created the following acronym—to remind you that, with practice, learning to transform your life can be as easy as learning your ABCs!

"A" is for Your New AGREEMENT TOOL

Today, I *(fill in your name)* make a commitment to focus ONLY ON MYSELF and the TRANSFORMED LIFE THAT I AM CREATING. This means I am NOW committed to do the ACTION STEPS for each chapter of this book. I NOW PROMISE MYSELF I will not get sidetracked by things that are not in alignment with my vision of my ideal life. I realize I do not have the time or energy to worry about or fix other people's lives, dramas, issues or obligations, nor is it my job to do so. My sole purpose is to improve my life, so I will NOT feel guilty about focusing on myself for (at least) the duration of this book! *(Note: even as a team player in your book club you are not focusing on other people! You're merely BELIEVING in one another and the visions each of you has for your new life.)*

Signature: _____

Date started book: _____

Date finished book: _____

"B" is for Your New BELIEF TOOL

From this moment forward, you are choosing to have a different BELIEF to create a NEW REALITY. You are, in essence, creating a different person from the one you were just a minute ago—that person who was stuck in unwanted drama, problems or issues. That person and those issues are no longer your reality, because you NOW have a new choice. Repeat this out loud: "That was the old me, this is the NEW ME!" Now, doesn't that feel good to say?

The first time I said that statement out loud I was at my psychiatrist's office. We had spent the last two years trying ten different antidepressants and so far nothing had helped with my postpartum depression and severe anxiety.

Earlier that morning, as I was getting ready for my appointment, I had decided I was done feeling like crap and whatever antidepressant she put me on this month was going to be my "silver bullet," the answer to my depression. I was ready to get on with my life.

My doctor had two chairs in her office, and normally I sat in the one closer to the door. But not that day. This was the NEW Bernadette and faced with the same situations I was going to make different choices than the ones the old Bernadette would have made.

If the doctor noticed that I had, for the first time, chosen the chair closer to her, she didn't say anything. Instead, she asked, "How are you doing on this current medicine?"

"I'm ready to try a different medicine," I replied matter-of-factly, "and I've decided whatever you give me today is going to be the answer I've been looking for, because *that was the old me and this is the NEW ME.*" (FYI: The old me had bad reactions to, or no positive effect from, the medications she prescribed.)

I will never forget the look on the doctor's face when I said those words; her eyes got really big, like she had just seen a ghost. She didn't respond right away, and I think she was debating whether or not I had finally gone off the deep end. When she found her voice, she said, "Okay this is what I am going to do for you…" (The medication she prescribed that day was not the perfect answer for me, but the next prescription was. Since then I have not had any issues with depression or anxiety.)

Now it's your turn to release any problems you've had in the past, including whatever your story was before, because from this moment forward *it is no longer your story*. You now choose this NEW BELIEF and MOTTO: "That was the old me, this is the NEW ME!"

Any time something isn't going your way and you realize you're repeating old patterns or old beliefs that you no longer want to be true, just stop yourself from talking or thinking or agreeing that this kind of negative stuff or situation "always happens to me."

Then say or think one of the following:

"I cancel and delete what I just said."

"Wait, let me find a more positive way to say that."

"Whoops, I almost forgot! That was the old me talking and NOW, as the NEW ME, I choose a better belief about _____." (Fill in with whatever positive situation you would rather have).

You will be amazed by how powerful those words are, especially when you say them out loud. People around you will stop and listen to the NEW YOU, and then they start to AGREE and BELIEVE IN THE NEW YOU TOO! It's almost as if you've created another Miracle Team, all because you decided that you will no longer accept and expect the old ways of living you once considered "normal."

As promised, here is my favorite example of how an ABSOLUTE BELIEF about oneself can cause instantaneous physiological changes. It involves people with Dissociative Identity Disorder (formerly Multiple Personality Disorder), in which a person's personality splits off into separate identities, each with a distinct background, habits and *beliefs*. The alternate personalities can even be of a different ethnicity or gender than the host. There have been numerous studies and theories about the disorder, and though there is still much to be learned scientists have found that it often begins as a defense mechanism to trauma, usually childhood trauma. My focus here, however, is on the cases of dramatic biological changes in these people as they switched from one personality to another. For example, if the host personality BELIEVES it is allergic to orange juice, the body, upon ingesting the juice, will break out in hives. However, if another personality was to take control, even during the allergic reaction, and that alternate personality BELIEVED IT WAS NOT allergic to orange juice, the hives would immediately go away. There have also been cases where one personality was diabetic and another showed no evidence of the disease, and still others when eye color changed depending upon which personality was in control. Other examples include the abrupt appearance and disappearance of rashes, welts, scars, and other tissue wounds; changes in handwriting and dexterity preferences, epilepsy, vision/blindness, allergies and colorblindness. [1]

This is fascinating stuff, but what really inspired me was that this phenomenon has been documented by scientists. This is proof that if we TRULY BELIEVE something about our bodies, our bodies will reflect that belief.

[1]Goleman, Daniel, "New Focus on Multiple Personality." Retrieved from https://www.nytimes.com/1988/06/28/science/probing-the-enigma-of-multiple-personality.html

THIS IS BECAUSE IF YOUR MIND TELLS YOUR BODY SOMETHING, YOUR BODY AUTOMATICALLY BELIEVES IT'S TRUE! For me this was absolutely life-changing. Whenever a hive would appear or symptoms of a cold started, instead of freaking out or saying, "Here we go again," I would instead say, **"This is not real and has NO POWER OVER ME. I am healthy, and my skin is clear and healthy. I FEEL GOOD FROM THE INSIDE AND OUT!"** Then I simply would not give any more energy to it and would busy myself doing something else that made me feel good and got my mind off it. I'm not saying the issue went away instantaneously, but I often would wake up the next day symptom-free and perfectly healthy, feeling good from the inside out!

"C" is for CREATING the Ideal You TOOL

You are Now creating a new, different picture in your mind of who you are and what your current reality looks like, per your IDEAL TRANSFORMED MIRACULOUS LIFE! You've always had this ability, and whether you know it or not, you've been using it every minute of every day—this is how you've created your life, both the positive and negative aspects, up to this point. Once you understand that you have used this POWER to create your present circumstances, you will come to the profound realization, as I did, that you have the power to CHANGE that reality into what you desire.

This power is well-known to Olympians and other athletes, who use mental imagery to maximize their performance on the field, the track, or in the boxing ring, et cetera. They understand that visualizing themselves playing the game or running the marathon, and incorporating their five senses into this imagery, has the same effect on the brain as if they were actually doing the activity. They are creating a roadmap for success, because the mind cannot tell the difference between visualization and actual participation.

Of course, the same is true for negative visualization. I know, because I used my power that way for the first twenty-five years of my life. Since I was always having health problems, I was overly aware of health issues in those around me, and I would often visualize what I would do if I got the flu or a cold or whatever was going around. Then I would be obsessed with negative thoughts of worst-case scenarios, such as "What if the doctors can't figure out this or that kind of problem with me?" And guess what, I continued to have issues with my health! I IMAGINED AND CONSTANTLY SAID, "If it's not one thing with my health it's another!"

Just understanding this empowered me to visualize health in my body and CREATE A NEW HEALTHY REALITY FOR EVERY AREA OF MY LIFE, and you can do it too! Let's begin creating your Ideal Vision for your life!

*To **BELIEVE** in a new vision for your life, you must **EXPERIENCE** it in your mind first.*

WEEK THREE ACTIVATION STEPS: YOUR TURN

Throughout this book we have been discussing how your BELIEFS create your reality—physically, mentally and spiritually. Now it's time to use this information to TRANSFORM and EMPOWER your life! Today, you can RELEASE your old story and every problem you had in the past and CHOOSE TO CREATE A NEW STORY in alignment with your desires. First ask yourself, what do you want this life to look like? Remember, this is the time to Dream Big, Bold and Unapologetically! (Don't forget to first PLUG IN to your Higher Source Energy and ask for Guidance.) Envision what your life would be like if you weren't worried about how much education you have (or don't have); how much money you need; a current medical diagnosis, et cetera. The list of limiting beliefs could go on forever, but they have no place in the infinite, miraculous possibilities you are NOW ACTIVATING, EXPECTING and ACCEPTING in order to create YOUR IDEAL TRANSFORMED LIFE!

First ACTION STEP: Your New Ideal Life Vision

Answer the following questions below. Take your time and be sure to use all five senses, for these details will help align your conscious and unconscious mind to work together. For example, what do you SEE and HEAR? Can you SMELL any new fragrances in the air or TASTE a particular flavor? What does it FEEL like to be living this Dream Come True?

1) Imagine Your Ideal Life. Envision yourself getting up and out of bed in the morning and looking forward to your day. Where will you go and what will you be doing?

_____
_____
_____
_____
_____
_____
_____
_____
_____
_____
_____
_____
_____
_____
_____
_____
_____
_____
_____
_____
_____
_____
_____
_____
_____
_____
_____
_____
_____
_____
_____

2) What do your personal and professional relationships look and feel like?

_____

_____

_____

_____

_____

_____

_____

_____

_____

_____

_____

_____

_____

_____

_____

_____

_____

_____

_____

_____

_____

_____

_____

_____

_____

_____

_____

_____

_____

3) Do you want to live a quiet life of peace and harmony, or do you want to have exciting new experiences each day? Describe in detail.

_____

_____

_____

_____

_____

_____

_____

_____

_____

_____

_____

_____

_____

_____

_____

_____

_____

_____

_____

_____

_____

_____

_____

_____

_____

_____

_____

_____

_____

_____

_____

_____

4) What does the IDEAL YOU look like and feel like? Is your hair the same color and cut? Are you same weight? What style of clothing does the ideal you wear? How does your body feel, is it more energetic or calmer, et cetera?

_____

_____

_____

_____

_____

_____

_____

_____

_____

_____

_____

_____

_____

_____

_____

_____

_____

_____

_____

_____

_____

_____

_____

_____

_____

5) What does your health look and feel like? Are there things your body can do NOW that it wasn't able to do before?

_____

_____

_____

_____

_____

_____

_____

_____

_____

_____

_____

_____

_____

_____

_____

_____

_____

_____

_____

_____

_____

_____

_____

_____

_____

_____

_____

_____

_____

_____

_____

6) What does your financial life look like? Imagine your new bank balance, and that all of your bills are now paid in full. What have you always wanted to buy for yourself now that you have the money to do so?

_____

_____

_____

_____

_____

_____

_____

_____

_____

_____

_____

_____

_____

_____

_____

_____

_____

_____

_____

_____

7) Where do you live and what does that look like in your life?

_____

_____

_____

_____

_____

_____

_____

_____

_____

_____

_____

_____

_____

_____

_____

_____

_____

_____

_____

_____

_____

_____

_____

_____

_____

_____

_____

_____

8) Is there anything else you want your IDEAL LIFE to include? These questions are just to get you thinking and to become a starting point that you will revise and improve as you expand your vision. The possibilities are truly endless!

_____

_____

_____

_____

_____

_____

_____

_____

_____

_____

_____

_____

_____

_____

_____

_____

_____

_____

_____

_____

_____

_____

_____

_____

_____

_____

_____

Second ACTION STEP: Your Visual Anchor

Use your answers to Questions 1-8 to guide you in creating a vision board. I personally love vision boards because they are POWERFUL VISUAL REMINDERS that the NEW YOU is only a vision away! If you're not familiar with this tool, it is when you take pictures and words (from magazines, newspapers, printed off the internet, et cetera) that symbolize what you want your life to look like and paste them onto a poster board. You can also find a vision board app and download it to your computer and phone, but I personally prefer to use the poster board because there's something about touching it with my hands and cutting out the pictures that makes it feel more real for me. I do take a picture of it with my phone and save it as my "wallpaper" so I am seeing it several times throughout the day. As you create your vision board, remember—this is a *fun* activity. It's not about being "realistic" about your life or your future. IT'S ABOUT CREATING A MIRACULOUS REALITY YOU TRULY WANT, THAT LIGHTS YOU UP FROM THE INSIDE OUT!

This tool is so powerful because it creates a VISUAL ANCHOR that keeps you on track and aligned with your NEW VISION OF YOUR IDEAL LIFE. The trick is to look at your vision board OFTEN, using all five senses to IMAGINE AND ENVISION these pictures as real and a part of your reality. This works on the unconscious and subconscious levels of mind, affirming and reaffirming that your ideal life is not foreign or out of reach, but possible and yours for the receiving. Eventually, it becomes EXPECTED.

"Think the thought until you believe it, and once you believe it, it is."

—Abraham Hicks

Third ACTION STEP: You Share

Once you have created your vision board, be sure to hang it in a place where you will see it daily, the more often the better, so you can visualize the items on it becoming a reality. Keep adding to your vision board as your ideas expand and you accept the endless possibilities that are available to you. Remember, THE DETAILS in this new vision make it more crystal clear, which solidify it in your conscious and unconscious mind!

Share your vision board with your Miracle Team because their BELIEF in you and their desire to see you succeed is a very powerful ingredient in helping your vision to become a reality. *As each member shares their vision board, the other team members visualize them accomplishing their dreams come true.* **From this moment forward, the team members are going to help one another "Cancel and Delete" any negative words they may unconsciously be using about their life vision so that they can reframe and restate it in a POSITIVE way that becomes a SELF-FULFILLING PROPHECY.**

"If you can SEE it in your MIND you will be able to HOLD it in your HAND."

—Bob Proctor

A Note about Sharing:

DO NOT SHARE your vision board with anybody who is negative or a naysayer. Just as positive reinforcement from others can accelerate your miracles, negative comments and energy are not helpful and in fact can be detrimental in these beginning stages. Remember, your job now is to create a life you can BELIEVE in, so that you can RECEIVE it.

On a Personal Note:

I keep my vision board in my own closet so as I get dressed and ready each morning, I can look at the pictures and visualize myself in the future I want. This is also a safe place, away from the eyes of disbelievers. As an empath I often feel what others are thinking, and I don't like feeling their disbelief when I look in their eyes or "see" the questions in their hearts about my vision board (i.e., "Where are you going to get the money to do all this?"; "Didn't you hear the doctor?"; "Do you expect me to provide this for you?" and so on).

Instead of exhausting myself by trying to explain that "the new miracle me I envision is activated by my vision board," I would rather spend that energy building myself up with BE-LIEVING energy! That's why I suggest sharing it only with your Miracle Team and other likeminded people.

The vision you have for your life is not for others to understand, because it is NOT their vision; it is YOURS!

That was the
Old Me

This is
The *New* Me!

I am in the *Process*

of

Positive Changes

in

EVERY AREA

of my *Life!*

✂

Chapter 4

Your New "Double Ds!"

*Y*ou are now preparing for your TRANSFORMED LIFE as if it is already "DD"—DONE DEAL!

Even if you cannot actually see it in your reality—yet! —this DONE DEAL thinking and believing creates a pathway for your miracles to easily come into your life. Each chapter of this book builds a new belief system, as it disrupts your old way of thinking and reprograms your expectations for allowing miracles in your life. This chapter guides you to agree to BELIEVE and have FAITH that there's a SOLUTION, MIRACLE, ANSWER-ED PRAYER, BETTER LIFE, DIVINE INTERVENTION—in other words, a MIRACULOUS TRANSFORMED LIFE—that is waiting just for you because anything less is no longer acceptable!

BELIEVING is the beacon that calls your MIRACLE into MANIFESTATION.

How to Believe in a DONE DEAL

That is the question I get asked most often by my workshop participants: "How do I believe in something better for my life when I feel like crap now or everything in my life is the complete opposite of what I want it to be?" The following three tools are the answer to this question!

The Believe in Miracles TOOL

In order to be able to EXPECT a miracle solution to your situation, you must first ACCEPT that miracles happen every day, all over the world, and NOW IT'S YOUR TURN!

The Universe and your Higher Power have been waiting for you to choose a REALITY different from the one you have currently decided is true in your life. As we discussed earlier, you must first identify and visualize what this ideal reality looks like; this NEW TRUTH must also be BELIEVABLE to you. From that belief, it is just a short leap to EXPECTING it to show up—this is DONE DEAL thinking. Life is exactly how you wanted it but, then again, you always knew it would be!

To begin this process, you need to immerse yourself in what I call "The Miracle Mindset World." This is a place where miracles happen everywhere, every day, and it's where I go when I am creating a new BELIEF in my life. This means that in every moment of my time that I am in control of (i.e. outside of work), I am laser-focused on what I listen to and watch, as well as who I surround myself with. In other words, I only allow into my world things and people that make me feel good and/or help me believe in miracles. I *do not have time* for anyone or anything that is negative *until my miracle has arrived.* My mantra during this time is "I NOW LIVE AND BREATHE MIRACLES ONLY!"

"If you always do what you've always done, you always get what you've always gotten."

-Jessie Potter

Again, this is why having a Miracle Team is so important. It creates a safe space where you can share with one another positive stories, miracles and/or "wins," and anything else you are doing that's in alignment with your ideal vision, which in turn encourages you to expect, both individually and collectively, more positive miraculous things to continue happening. *REMEMBER: When two or more people agree to come together for a common theme, the extra attention and intention amplifies the positively and accelerates the appearance of miracles!*

Omit Miracle-Blocking Habits:

DO NOT read sad things or watch negative movies, T.V. shows, Facebook posts, commercials, or news stories. If you must be up to date on the news, find a news channel or radio station that reports current events in a neutral way (as opposed to angry opinion shows). And though I approach the information and tools in this book in a religion-neutral way, I must point out an excellent (and all too rare) example: Christian radio stations. They constantly pump feel-good stories through the airwaves, including those I don't hear anywhere else. When they do report on a negative world event, they come at it from a positive perspective, such as a call to action to pray for those affected. After listening to this kind of news reporting I actually have hope for those situations, which is very important for someone who is healing or needing to UPLEVEL THEIR POSITIVE ENERGY to call in their MIRACLES!

And, as mentioned earlier, do not engage or entertain negative people during this time because you don't want to "catch" their negativity. Emotion Contagion (EC), as it is called by social scientists, is the tendency for people to unconsciously and automatically mimic the emotional expressions of others. During this time it is imperative that you make your mental health a priority and your environment ONLY POSITIVE. The rule of thumb is that if something has the potential to make you concentrate on what you are trying to "un-believe"; shake your belief in your miracle; make you feel bad or sad; or confront you with any of "the harsh realities of life," eliminate it from your experience IMMEDIATELY!

Your NEW REALITY is, "I live in a world where miracles happen every day and NOW

IT IS MY TURN FOR MIRACLES!"

Practice Miracle-Creating Rituals

Miracle Mindset World is not just about avoiding the negative; it is also a time for embracing the positive and having fun. Spend every moment you can listening, watching and interacting with things and people that uplift your spirit and strengthen your belief that your miracles are arriving NOW. Here are my personal favorites:

Movies

- *The Secret* (based on the book of the same name by Rhonda Byrne). This beginner's guide to the Law of Attraction is jam-packed with many true stories of miracles come true. (If you really want to be blown away, look for the story about the "Miracle MAN"!)
- *Invincible.* This is a true story of Vince Papale (played by Mark Wahlberg), a thirty-year-old bartender from South Philadelphia who beats the odds to play for the Philadelphia Eagles in 1976. This is an amazing story, and even if you don't like football (like me) you will be inspired by seeing him at his "darkest before his dawn!"
- *McFarland, USA.* This is the true story of a track team at an economically challenged school in California that overcomes great odds to become champion runners. Kevin Costner plays Jim White, the real-life coach who sees the bigger picture and serves as the motivating force for the team. I personally can watch this movie over and over even though I'm not into sports.

Books

- *Dying to be Me*, by Anita Moorjani. This is the incredible true story of a woman's near-death experience. Moorjani, whose body was riddled with cancer, had slipped into a coma and suddenly found herself standing outside her body. After communicating with her father and her best friend, both of whom had passed away years earlier, she was given the choice to remain on the other side or resume her life on earth. Moorjani chose the latter and made a full recovery from her cancer. Her message to the world is that we have nothing to fear, for love is all there is, AND it's never too late to heal completely!

- *You Can Heal Your Life,* by Louise Hay. Considered by many to be the seminal book on self-healing, it is a favorite of mine because it provides specific emotional causes for a variety of physical illnesses. This book started me on my healing journey and I refer to it often!

Audio

I listen to anything positive—CDs, audiobooks, or podcasts— while I'm doing chores or errands that don't require concentration. One of my favorite people to listen to is Joel Osteen, a charismatic Christian minister whose message is very aligned with spiritual teachings. Though I don't believe his objective is to reach the "spiritual but not religious" crowd, this is precisely what he has done, attracting millions of people of all religions and belief systems from around the world. Joel is my absolute go-to whenever I need to be reminded that I am only a belief away from my miracle! I play his book audible in my car radio and by the time I get to my next appointment I already believe MY MIRACLE IS A DONE DEAL!

Other

Don't forget about the standard things that help you feel good from the inside out, like eating healthy, exercising, hanging out with positive friends, and doing anything that feeds your soul and makes you feel carefree. It is during those moments of fun, when you're living in the moment and not worrying about your situation or what you're going to do next, that the answers come to you. This is when you're *naturally* PLUGGED IN and it's easiest to see, hear or feel YOUR NEXT BEST STEP. Yes, I'm saying doing things that make you feel good also helps to get your prayers answered faster! Contrary to what your logical mind might think, all work and no play does not help your prayers get answered faster, *even if you're praying for more money.* You still need to go to work every day and work as hard as you can, but don't forget to salt-and-pepper your days with things that feel good like watching the sunset and playing with your kids, because this is when your Higher Power and your soul will speak to you about your miracles and what to do to get there. I know that sounds too good to be true, but don't worry; I will explain this in more depth in a couple of pages.

Your Words are Your Wand

This is so simple you won't believe it! I actually mentioned it in the introduction but you might have been so eager to get to the "good stuff" that you missed it. In fact, this is the "good stuff," and the most important TOOL to activate your miracles. Here it is: THINK and TALK about ONLY what you WANT to be TRUE. Because with every thought you think and every word you say you are announcing to the Universe what you EXPECT, CONFIRM, ACCEPT AND WANT MORE OF IN YOUR LIFE! Your words are truly your wands, so stop using them to create what you do not want and start using them to ACTIVATE your ideal future.

"What we THINK ABOUT, we TALK ABOUT. What we TALK ABOUT, we BRING ABOUT!" [2]

Why Something So Simple is So Hard to Do

Most people don't really listen to themselves think or talk, so they don't realize how often they focus on negative issues in their life. It is always easier to see other people's negativity than it is to see our own. Let's begin with an example everybody can relate to. Think of a friend or family member who is always sick or always having negative things happen to them. Now think about your last visit with this person and answer these following questions to yourself.

- Did this person talk about their illness or negative situation?
- Did they talk for only a little bit about their negative situation, or did they *hijack* the conversation and make it *all* about their situation?
- Did this person ask you about yourself? If so, was the conversation equally balanced with information about you and information about them? Did the two of you talk about positive aspects more often than not during this conversation, or was the tone mostly negative?
- Did you try to offer some kind of positive solution for their issue and they ONLY had a negative response of WHY NOTHING WOULD or COULD work for them?
- Did you want to stay and visit with this person forever OR did you get away as quickly as possible and hope it would be forever before you had to visit them again?

---

[2] Rohm, Robert, PhD. "What you think about and talk about, you bring about!" Personality Insight. https://www.personality-insights.com/tip-what-you-think-about-and-talk-about-you-bring-about/

The above is an extreme example of "What we think about, we talk about and what we talk about, we bring about!" When we are around this type of negative person, we can easily begin to feel or relate to similar health issues or dramas in our own life and before we know it we are concentrating on those negative issues and aspects. Remember, negativity is contagious! When I'm around a person like this, it feels like I'm being brainwashed because I easily begin to feel and agree with the other person's hopelessness. I often feel yucky, like I should go home and take a shower to wash off their negativity!

The Old Me:

I hate to say it, but I was definitely that kind of negative person you didn't want to be around, and my negativity got worse before it got better! For some reason I just couldn't wait to share all my horrible health experiences with whoever would listen, even though talking about it made me feel worse and more hopeless (though I'll admit that sometimes it also made me feel good to get it all out into the open). Truth be told, I was so consumed with the poor state of my health that I really had nothing else to talk to people about. *I'm happy to say it's been fifteen years since I've had those kind of health issues, and it all started to improve the moment I decided I was done with being sick all the time and I wanted to be healthy! I then STOPPED TALKING and THINKING about being sick and I started to apply the information in this book to my life. Now it's your turn!*

How to Call in Your Miracle TOOL

This has been the MOST POWERFUL TOOL for me to reprogram my negative thinking and living. It also helps to convince me that what I want is already a DONE DEAL. Best of all, I can do it anywhere, at any time, and so can you!

This tool involves using your words—your WANDS—to activate your miracles. Some people would say you're using "affirmations" or "declarations," but I'm not a big fan of those terms because they don't accurately convey the power of this tool. Instead, I use the term CALL IN, because it speaks to your ability to BRING YOUR MIRACLE TO YOU. We know that whatever comes out of our mouths was first experienced in our minds as thoughts. The problem is that most of the time we don't notice our own negative thoughts and words because we have become so comfortable with that state of being. Our Higher Power and The Universe, however, are always listening to every thought we think and every word we speak.

Think of this tool like a bullhorn in front of your mouth, blasting your thoughts and words out unto the world. These thoughts and words act like a POWERFUL MAGNET, attracting whatever you THINK or SAY (or it's energetic equivalent) to you.

When clients first start working with me, many will say they don't believe making positive statements can actually change their lives. After all, they've tried in the past with no success. When we delve deeper, I realize that the reason such statements didn't work for them is because they were doing it wrong; they were making it harder than it had to be. You don't need to write them down or remember long sentences!

The purpose of these statements is very simple: to preoccupy your brain with thinking about and talking about what you DO WANT instead of what you don't want. This essentially stops the broken record you've been playing in your head about how horrible your situation is, and reprograms that record to play something that takes you towards your miracle.

How to (Almost) Effortlessly Reprogram Your Thinking

The following prompts are my favorites because they're easy to use any time you need to replace a negative thought. Just make sure your statements are short, to the point, and stated in the present tense with positive language. Don't just say the statement once—keep repeating it in your mind until the broken record of negativity is replaced with something new and positive or you are distracted to something else that is more neutral.

"I am_____."

"I now have _____."

"I believe my miracle (insert your desire here) is a DONE DEAL!"

GRATITUDE STATEMENTS are a powerful amplifier and miracle accelerator. Use the below prompts whenever you want to draw your miracle to you even faster.

"I am so grateful for _____!"

"I am so thankful I am_____!"

"I am so blessed to have_____!"

"I love and appreciate my healthy, happy _____!"

"THANK YOU,_____(Fill in your Higher Power), for _____!"

How to Activate This in Everyday Life:

This tool should be used any time you catch yourself thinking or saying something that contradicts what you want to be true in your life. If you're like me, this can happen off and on throughout the day (when I'm feeling sorry for myself or in fear about a situation).

I introduced my son to this concept when he was three years old. At that time, he did not know I had hives covering my whole body and affected my life as much as they did. What he did know was, "Mama doesn't feel good," and I wanted to find a way to start our day on a positive note and to teach him the power of his thoughts and words. I explained in terms a child could understand, by saying, "I have a secret I just learned and I want to share it with you. Our thoughts and words are very powerful, and what we think and say throughout the day is like a prayer of what we want to be true in our life."

Then, as we drove to preschool or wherever we were going, we would sing short songs about what we wanted our reality to look like. We would each take turns, repeating it back to the other, thereby reinforcing our ideal vision. He just thought we were singing because it's fun to sing, but the truth was singing is actually a higher vibration which calls your miracles in faster!

I would begin singing, then he would repeat it back to me. Here are some of the statements we sang (though I would word them a bit differently each day):

- "I Now feel GOOD from the inside out!"
- "I BELIEVE I am healthy in every area of my life!"
- "I am wealthy in every area of my life!"
- "I am so HAPPY that my perfect health is A DONE DEAL!"

When it was my son's turn, he chose things like this:

- "I am big!"
- "I am strong!"
- "I am liked!"
- "I am healthy!"

I then would repeat each statement back to him.

We would do this for at least five to ten minutes until we ran out of ideas.

It was a fun way to start our day, and my son, now twenty (and big and strong) still remembers those car rides!

How to Speak Miracles in Everyday Life

Remember, we need to wield our wands (our words) in alignment with what we want our truth to be. To do this, we need to arm ourselves with words that we can use in daily situations. For example, the question "How are you doing?" is a standard greeting, so we can pretty much count on someone asking it at some point in our day. If you're feeling good, answering that question is easy enough; the problem comes in when you're feeling like crap. You don't want to enforce how negative you're currently feeling so you could use one of the following positive statements that reflect how you *do* want to feel.

- "I am feeling BETTER and BETTER every day, in every way."
- "I BELIEVE every area of life is in the process of HEALING NOW."
- "I am in the process of positive changes in every area of my life."
- "I am fabulous, how about you!"

Speak These When You Want to Call Your Miracle in With a Megaphone:

- "TODAY I am feeling SOOO GOOD. I know the prayer I have been praying for is a DONE DEAL I can just FEEL IT!"

The response I receive to that statement is always something like, "Tell me more! What were you praying for?" I always reply, "I'll tell you all about it the next time I see you!"

- "I am feeling miraculous today! How are you?"
- "I am a walking, talking, breathing miracle. Thank you for reminding me!"

These kind of fun replies always make me feel better than I did before I said them, and they usually evoke laughter from whoever I'm speaking with. Joy and laughter are so important for calling in your miracles, because feeling GOOD is LIGHT AND BRIGHT, just like miracles are, and remember, "like attracts like!" The other person will usually respond with something like, "You sound amazing!" or "I want that too! What do I need to do to have that?" I simply tell them, "Well, you are a miracle also. Sometimes we just forget it. That's why I'm SO GLAD you reminded me!"

NOTE: *Whenever you talk to your Miracle Team, it should be with these kind of positive remarks and everybody should join in with SEEING and BELIEVING and AGREEING that "Yes, it is a DONE DEAL and I can see it for you NOW!" Remember, this helps you build one another up with EXPECTANT, DONE DEAL ENERGY, which is exponentially more powerful than when you're conversing with somebody who does not know of or is not in agreement with your miracle.*

Create Longer Statements When You Need to Amp Up Your Activation

I prefer to do these longer statements when I am alone (i.e. while cleaning the house or driving around) because I can say them out loud. Don't be afraid to keep rewording until you feel it speaks the truth of what you are wanting. You'll know when it's right because it will feel so good and empowering!

Here are some examples:

"In my mind, from now on there is no other option than a miraculous solution for _____ !"

"I now believe the _____ I want is already a DONE DEAL!"

"I am now ready to receive _____, because I DO BELIEVE in MIRACLES!'

"I am so grateful for the NOW COMPLETE HEALING in my _____ !"

"I am so happily blessed with _____ in every area of my life!"

"I am so thankful that the miracle of _____ is now a DONE DEAL!"

Hints for Customizing Your Own Powerful Statements

These are mantras that you'll be repeating to yourself, your Higher Power and others around you about what you want and expect from your life from now on, so be sure to make them fun and easy to remember (i.e. something that rhymes or is sing-songy). **In the beginning, calling in your miracle may feel fake, but that's okay. The more you say it, the MORE BELIEVABLE it will**

become to you and then to the people around you. Eventually you all will start to not only believe it, but to EXPECT it.

If Others React Negatively to the Improved You

While making positive changes in your life, you may find that some friends or family members are not quite as excited as you are. In fact, they may not like the changes at all. This may be because they were comfortable with the way you have always been; they may have even unconsciously enjoyed being needed by you when you were not at your best in terms of health, wealth, happiness, et cetera. Or, they may still be playing that negative broken record in their own heads and are therefore having a hard time believing in your positivity. Whatever the reason, you may hear something like, "I don't think you should be too optimistic. I don't want you to be disappointed if that doesn't happen."

This can feel like a punch to a gut in the beginning, but know that you have a CHOICE here—you can allow their words to derail you, or you can say something like, "You are welcome to your opinion and so am I"; or, "That may be your truth, but it is not my truth anymore." Then *change the subject,* because there is no reason to have a conversation about this. You are not trying to change their beliefs; you are only HEALING YOUR OWN BELIEFS so that you can have the transformed life you truly want.

Prepare for Your Miracle(s) Because It's a DONE DEAL TOOL

This tool is all about complete and utter BELIEF that your affirmations/prayers/call-in statements have already been answered, even if you do not see that at the moment. My favorite way to remind myself and get in the right frame of mind is to insert myself in the story of the two farmers. I have heard this story in many different contexts, but my favorite is in *Facing the Giants*, another football movie in which the main character, Coach Taylor, undergoes spiritual and professional trials while taking his team to victory. In the movie, another character, Mr. Bridges, tells the story to the coach.

"There're two farmers," Mr. Bridges says, "who desperately needed rain, and both of them prayed for rain. But only one of them went out and prepared his fields to receive it.

Which one do you think trusts God to send the rain?"

"The one who prepared his fields for it?" Coach Taylor asks.

"Which one are you?" Bridges replies, "God will send the rain when He is ready. You need to prepare your field to receive it."

I think about this story *every* time I'm ready for my issues to be over or for my desires to be a DONE DEAL. I imagine what would MY NEXT STEP BE, IF I WAS ALREADY LIVING MY MIRACLE OF my healthiest, wealthiest, ideal life that I have dreamed about and prayed for.

"It is better to BELIEVE than disbelieve. In doing so, you bring everything into the realm of POSSIBILITY." —Albert Einstein

When You're Not on the Same Page

This chapter has covered how to stay positive while establishing and maintaining your BELIEF in the arrival of your miracles, including what to do when you're confronted by negative people. But what about those who are desiring the same miracle(s) as you but for whatever reason do not share your belief in this way of thinking? Does this mean your prayers and call-ins won't work? ABSOLUTELY NOT. It does not matter if the people in your life agree with you, pray, or have the same beliefs as you. You need only do what you can do, and what your Higher Power guides you to do, every day. You also trust that Higher Power to guide the other people in the situation to do their part. I know this to be true from personal experience. As I mentioned in the beginning of the book, my husband and I have always had different beliefs about spirituality. However, when faced with challenges, we still formed a powerful team, each making our contribution to solve our problem and reach our goal. It is important to note that we did this without an agreed-upon plan and oftentimes without even knowing the specifics of what the other was doing or thinking.

How This TOOL Helped Us Keep Our House:

This was in the early part of our marriage (before my husband built the dream house I mentioned in Chapter 2). We had fallen on hard times and were about to lose our home, along with a rental property we were trying to sell and a piece of equipment my husband needed for his work. It was also when I was in the grips of depression and anxiety and, though I desperately wanted to help my husband pay the bills, I was unable to handle a job.

How My Husband UNKNOWINGLY Prepared His Fields for Rain:

During this time, my husband did everything humanly possible to bring more money into the house, namely, working seven days a week, sometimes for twelve to eighteen hours a day. Now, he could have pointed a finger at me and said it was all my fault that we were about to lose everything because I wasn't working. Or he could've given up and decided to just stay in bed because our situation felt and looked like a hopeless cause. If he chose those actions, we would have been working against one another and I believe we would have not had the positive results as quickly as we did. But he didn't; he chose instead to work as if that alone would bring in the money we needed. He was unknowingly "preparing his fields for the rain," and his efforts brought a miracle opportunity to us to bring in the money needed.

How I KNOWINGLY Prepared Our Fields for Rain:

I knew on a deep level that my husband would agree with the analogy of the farmer preparing for the rain—that was clear from the physical effort he was putting in. However, since he's not a religious or spiritual person, or one that believes in energy or the POWER of BEING POSITIVE and believing in a DONE DEAL, I didn't tell him what I was doing to prepare for our miracle.

Since I knew I was unable to do the physical work needed to pay bills, I did everything I possibly could do to shift the thoughts and beliefs that were contributing to the energy of fear, scarcity, lack and doubt in our home. When we received a thirty-day notice to vacate our house and bill collectors were calling every fifteen minutes, I didn't spend my days worrying and crying, though this would have been very easy to do! Instead, I CALLED IN our miracle. I envisioned and prepared for all our bills to be paid. I stopped avoiding the bill collectors' calls, which I had been doing for six months, and instead picked up the phone and told every single one of them what I WANTED OUR TRUTH to be: *"I was just about to call you and let you know we received word that the money we've been expecting is on its way. We will be receiving money from a rental property that we have just sold!"* Sometimes I would switch it up and say:

"My husband just finished a big job and we're receiving enough money to get caught up with everything we owe you. We are thinking it will only take about a week or so. Please note this on our account so we do not get any further calls this week. Thank you for your willingness to work with us on this."

This new way of talking felt so good and fun! Most importantly, the more I said it out loud, the more I began to believe what I was saying was true!

NOTE:

The reason I had the bill collectors note our account to stop calling was because every time the phone rang it was a reminder that we had not paid a bill. Since I was stepping into "MY MIRACLE MINDSET WORLD," I chose instead to omit any harsh realities that drew my thoughts and attention to the opposite of what I wanted to be true.

During this time, I also took extra care of our house. I began to clean and reorganize it to work more efficiently for us. I figured if I was not well enough (yet) mentally to get a job that we desperately needed, then I was going to love and prepare our house for a long, happy future with my family, because that is what I prayed for! I did whatever I could do to CONFIRM OUR HOUSE WOULD REMAIN OUR HOME! I would dust all our little knickknacks and pictures of our family, and as I touched each item I would speak gratitude over the house, for example, "I am so thankful that we are NOW PAID UP TO DATE with our mortgage in this safe and warm house." I would alternate this with health affirmations so that I could be mentally able to work ASAP! "I am feeling better and better, every day in every way, and I am now divinely guided to a perfect job for me!" I knew these affirmations were my prayers sent to the Universe and my Higher Power, declaring the divine intervention we needed. The physical acts—deep cleaning and organizing our house—were the ACTIVATION STEPS I took to seal the DONE DEAL that I wanted!

Stay in Your Miracle Mindset, NO MATTER WHAT

During this time a family member who knew about our situation called me up. When they asked what I was up to, I replied, "I'm cleaning and reorganizing my house." And when they said, "Shouldn't you be packing everything and getting ready to move out?" I replied, "No, we're expecting our money any day now and it will be enough to get us caught up on our bills!" Immediately, I could sense this relative's demeanor and energy toward me change. They now felt better about our situation and weren't worrying about us anymore, which is exactly what I wanted because ANY worried energy sent our way would not help our situation; it would only add to the energy of fear and lack I was working on omitting! On some deep level I knew that if other people believed in our miracle too IT WOULD HELP OUR MIRACLE FIND US FASTER!

Where there is HOPE, there are MIRACLES.

Notice Inner Guidance and Opportunities

The very same week that I started this way of thinking, talking and answering the phone without fear and dread, my husband was working at somebody's house, doing their concrete. One day, the woman of the household said to him, "My daughter is selling St. Patrick's Day raffle tickets for her Christian school and there's a chance to win ten thousand dollars. If you'd like to be in the drawing it's one ticket for five dollars or five tickets for twenty." My husband bought the five tickets and never told me. That weekend was St. Patrick's Day, which just happens to be my birthday, and on that day a woman called our house. My husband answered the phone, and I noticed that as she spoke to him his demeanor changed; he seemed odd and awkward, and I thought he must be talking to a salesperson.

When he hung up the phone, he said, "That woman said I won the raffle for ten thousand dollars." He then told me how he had purchased the five tickets earlier in the week. "I don't know if I believe her," he added, "Maybe the people I bought the ticket from are playing a trick on me? Let's call the school on Monday and see if this is true." My husband found it hard not to dwell or worry about this for the rest of the weekend. That kind of money could change our situation, and his thoughts ran to fear that it was too good to be true. However, that weekend wasn't hard for me because I knew without a doubt this was A DONE DEAL; the MIRACLE I had been asking for and preparing for was finally here!

Finally, Monday morning arrived. I called the school, heard the words confirming what I already knew: "Yes, you won the ten thousand dollars and you can pick up your check immediately!" I was so exhilarated because that check saved us from losing everything, and there were more miracles to come. Later that month our tenant came into the money he needed to buy the rental house from us!

WEEK FOUR ACTIVATION STEPS: HOW TO RECEIVE YOUR "DOUBLE DS"

First ACTION STEP: How to Believe

Find some miracles to BELIEVE in. Google true stories, books, movies, podcast, YouTube videos about miracles, then save them in your phone to look at whenever you have free time. Choose to consume ONLY POSITIVITY this week (or, even better, for the remainder of the book!). Don't forget to PLUG IN and ask your Inner Guidance for direction as to where and what info would be most inspiring for you. Then watch and listen for reappearing info, books, websites or ideas you are drawn to. Share all info you find with your TEAM MEMBERS so that these positive resources pack at least twice the punch.

Second ACTION STEP: Call in Your Miracles

Create one or two positive statements that you will automatically say when someone says, "How are you doing today?" or "What's new in your life?" Remember, you may feel like a robot when you first utter these replies. This is okay, because your brain and body work like a computer and you are reprogramming them to invite and receive the BEST outcomes. It can even be fun! Here is a great ACTION STEP to practice with your TEAM MEMBERS so that you all get comfortable with your wording until it FEELS TRUE to you. Texting one another and asking how you're doing every day is a fun way to try out new statements to CALL IN YOUR MIRACLES. This way, when a family member or friend asks you how you're doing, you have already programmed your brain with ready-to-go, positive responses that feel effortlessly true!

Third ACTION STEP: Prepare for Your DONE DEAL

Imagine the ideal life you're creating is true right now, or right around the corner. What would your next step be to draw it even closer, faster?

EXAMPLE: Steps to Do Alone or With Your Team

First, choose something you want to bring into your reality—for example, a nice beach vacation—that you don't have the funds for (yet!). Now, "go shopping" on Amazon, placing a bunch of items you would like for the trip in the "save for later" area of your cart—*with the intention to actually buy them later*. Or, look for a new swimsuit you hope to wear on your trip, then start that new diet that will give you the body you are looking forward to showing off at the beach. If you're wanting to buy a new house but don't have the credit you need, speak to a mortgage specialist and ask them what steps you need to take to improve your credit. Then go to open houses in the neighborhoods you would love to live in and in each house imagine where your furniture would go or how you would paint the walls.

It doesn't matter that you are not actually spending the money right now. This is all about preparing your MIND and FEELING EXCITED that the TRANSFORMED LIFE you are wanting is TRUE or ALMOST HERE!

A DONE DEAL

in my *Mind*

creates

a DONE DEAL

in my *Life!*

✂

My *Miracle* of IDEAL (fill in the blank)

is only a *Belief* away

Where it is

a DONE *Deal*

waiting for me!

✂

Chapter 5

Receiving Magically in Your Life

*I*magine you have come to see me at an event where I am speaking to a room of two hundred people. During my talk I ask for a participant from the audience, then I choose a full-figured, stocky, short woman wearing a tight, neon lime-green polka dot dress. I'll call her "Helga." When she joins me on the brightly-lit stage, I hand Helga the local newspaper and ask her to read an article to herself while she stands there. I then turn to the audience and say:

"You are NOT going to like what I'm going to ask you to do, but in order for this exercise to work you need to follow my directions exactly.

"As you watch Helga reading the newspaper, I want you to think negative things about her, for example, "I hate her shoes," or "That's an ugly dress," et cetera. These thoughts do not need to be true or things you believe. Just *pretend* you mean it! You will all do this for one minute, while our onstage participant concentrates on reading the newspaper. The alarm will ring when one minute is up."

We do this twice, but the second time I whisper something in Helga's ear before we begin.

The Following are Actual Results from This Real Exercise I Use in My Workshops:

When I asked the audience and "Helga" how they felt and what they noticed during the first minute, people from the audience made comments like,

"I was uncomfortable!"

"I felt horrible!"

"It was the longest minute of my life!"

"I had a hard time thinking of negative thoughts!"

Helga said things like:

"I couldn't concentrate to read!"

"My thoughts felt foggy!"

"I had a hard time standing, I felt like I was being pushed backwards!"

NOTE: Every participant had some kind of PHYSICAL EXPERIENCE. The audience also noticed this reaction, saying that they could actually see the participant swinging back and forth as if he/she could not stand still while reading. It was almost as if the participant was dizzy.

After the second minute, I asked them again. Comments from the audience included:

"This time was even harder!"

"I couldn't concentrate!"

"I had a hard time thinking of things to be negative about!"

"The time felt longer then the first minute!"

Helga, on the other hand, said:

"I felt stronger and had no problem standing!"

"I felt good!"

"The time went by fast!"

Remember how before the start of the second minute I whispered something in Helga's ear?

What could I have said to make her experience so completely different from the first?

I told her that during the second minute she and I were going to send positive thoughts and/or love and light to the audience, for example: "I bless you and send you love"; "I ask the angels to surround you with love and light"; or "I am thankful for you." I also told her we could look at different people in the audience and think positive things like; "I like your haircut" or "What a lovely outfit you're wearing"—basically anything positive she could think of, EVEN IF SHE WAS MAKING IT UP!

The most amazing thing about this exercise is that we don't have to FEEL or BELIEVE these positive thoughts; we just have to INTEND them, just as the audience did not have to mean any of their negative thoughts toward Helga. They only had to intend them, yet she still felt the effects. Of course, if you do mean it and believe it, the results are even more intense!

I love to use this example because it reminds people how powerful their thoughts are. Our negative thoughts can actually make us sick or not feel good; they also negatively affect the object of those thoughts. Moreover, these thoughts do nothing to improve whatever or whoever you're complaining about; it actually makes the situation worse!

Consider this the next time someone is working below your

expectations (i.e. not performing well at your office), or you're in line at the grocery store and think the cashier is taking too long. Instead of thinking, "OMG, this person is taking forever and not very good at their job, this company should fire them!" instead choose thoughts that are good, positive, and with the intent to help, such as:

"This cashier must have had a long day. I'm going to send her positive thoughts that she easily and effortlessly adjusts to the rush of customers that just sprang up out of nowhere. Also, I'm sending positive thoughts to the others who work here, so that they will open more registers and take some stress off of this beautiful woman!"

Or,

"I just noticed that shade of blue she is wearing really accentuates her eyes. I'm going to let her know that as soon as I get to the register, which will be any minute!"

Or,

I just noticed she was really efficient with that last customer. There's only three more people before me. I'll be out of here in no time!"

The Secret Weapon TOOL

Think ONLY about what you want to be true, even when it involves other people, because IT ACTUALLY HELPS THEM DO BETTER! At the very least, find something positive about them, then only think about that to get your mind off the negative thoughts you are tempted to dwell on.

Your thoughts can build people up or tear them down. It doesn't matter if you say them out loud or think them, or whether you mean them or you don't, because energetically IT IS ALL THE SAME.

Most of us focus the bulk of our negativity on ourselves, often without thinking about it and because we simply don't realize how poisonous these thoughts are to our wellbeing. Take a minute to reflect on how you treat yourself. For example, when you look in the mirror do you find yourself thinking or saying things like:

"I hate being overweight (or underweight, or too tall, too short, et cetera)!"

"I wish I had a bigger_____ or a littler _____."

"As soon as my_____ is better, I will find my perfect _____!"

Through your negative body talk and thoughts you are unconsciously SABOTAGING your goals for a healthier body, while at the same time creating a SELF-FULFILLING PROPHECY that you do not want to be true.

Negative self-talk is exponentially more damaging when your body is experiencing a health crisis, whether it's something major like cancer or diabetes, or something relatively minor like a cold or the flu. That said, hating or being angry at your own body is ALWAYS the worst possible thing you could do and will

NEVER help your body heal, experience a miracle or motivate you, consciously or unconsciously, to make the positive changes you want or need to transform or create a healing.

The Miracle Magnet TOOL

We've discussed how thinking and saying ONLY positive things about others can have an amazing effect on both their day and yours. However, it is when you combine this with thinking and saying ONLY positive stuff about yourself that the magic happens! *Why? Because when you do these things every day you begin to feel better and behave differently.* You naturally smile more often, and there's a glow and good feeling that just seems to emanate from you. Friends and family will begin asking you what is new because you seem so different. Strangers will go out of their way to help you, you will get the best service wherever you go, and parking places open up just when you arrive. You become a positive circumstances attractor and MIRACLE MAGNET, all from changing your thoughts and words!

LOVE or a POSITIVE INTENTION are MAGNETS for MIRACLES, because what you GIVE OUT to the world is what you GET BACK.

The First Time I Sent Love Intentions, I Was FURIOUS

My husband and I had been married for ten years when we found ourselves facing a serious crisis in our relationship. For about six months we had been fighting on and off had even mentioned the possibility of divorce. One day, I asked him to help me hang up pictures in our front room. He said yes, but it was the last thing he wanted to do at the moment and we wound up fighting about where we should place the pictures. The conversation became heated, and I realized I had a choice to make. Instead of staying there and arguing, I told him to forget about the pictures; I then left the room, went to the other side of the house and immediately began sending him a beautiful, pink light filled with love. Though I was very angry, crying, and at that moment *not* feeling love for my husband, I imagined this light surrounding him. I also asked my Higher Power to magnify this loving intention to create true, unconditional healing love. I only thought about this for a couple of minutes while I calmed myself down, then I did something to keep myself busy and get my mind off it.

Within fifteen minutes my husband came into the room I was in and apologized to me. *This was the first time in our marriage he had ever done this on his own!* For me this was a major turning point in our relationship and the start of the healing I had CALLED IN a few moments earlier. This was incontrovertible proof that love—or at least the intention of love—could heal my marriage, and it did! We have now been married for twenty years and my husband just commented the other day that he cannot remember the last time we fought. We both decided it was several years ago!

It Only Takes One

As mentioned throughout this book, you have the ability to activate miracles for yourself and someone else, even if they are not on the same page, energetically speaking, as you. This was certainly the case in the above example. I decided to set the intention to bring about healing for our marriage, *regardless of my husband's feelings at that time.* I expressed this intention by sending him unconditional MAGNIFIED love whenever I thought of him or found myself wishing that aspects of our relationship were better or different. *Most importantly, I did this when we were fighting or my feelings were hurt, so that I could shift my energy and focus on what I wanted to be true.*

> Note: Do NOT expect the relationship or the person to change IMMEDIATELY. Just mind your thoughts and words using the tools in this book and HOPE and BELIEVE in the healing!

Use the "F Word"

When you find it hard (or nearly impossible) to send even the intention of love or good thoughts to someone or a situation, most likely the "F word" is an underlining issue for you. No, I am not talking about the expletive, but about FORGIVENESS. A book about miracles is not complete without a section on forgiveness. I know that after reading this some of you are ready to skip this section or close the book altogether because whoever or whatever did you wrong does not deserve to be forgiven!

The problem with that idea is you are the one that pays for this unforgiveness in the long run, through your illnesses, constant dramas, a lack of healthy relationships, or whatever your Achilles' heel might be.

Think back to the story of Helga and my workshops. What we send out into the world through thoughts or words comes back to us, and the fact that we think "good thoughts" most of the time does not make us immune to the effects of any lousy thoughts we may have. This means we cannot make exceptions for that one person, organization, religious group or political party that we deem unforgivable. This is not about condoning another's behavior or beliefs, but about making the choice to not give any more of your energy and time to condemning them. Remember, your focus should be on what you WANT TO EXPERIENCE, not on the impossible task of changing others.

When you're tempted to go down this road, remember: your constant dislike of another affects you even more than it affects them. And the lack of forgiveness is often what is BLOCKING you from your miracle.

I Had Nothing to Lose

When I first heard of this concept, I had already overcome my depression and the possibility of losing our house. However, I soon found myself in the thralls of the new condition—the hives that took over my body at will. My husband and I also had a new, larger financial goal, that of having enough money to pay off that house completely so we could move and build our dream home. This baffled me. I couldn't understand why or how I had overcome so many challenges, only to be confronted in a matter of months with a new set of challenges that were eerily similar (i.e. one was related to health and the other to money). As I pondered this situation, I started thinking about forgiveness, specifically the belief that if you don't forgive others who have done you wrong, you will remain stuck in an endless cycle of whatever it is you do not want. The act of forgiveness, on the other hand, clears the path to your miracle. Marianne Williamson, who is one of my favorite spiritual teachers, has this to say about the subject: "Forgiveness is the choice to see people as they are now. When we're mad at people, we're angry because of something they said or did before this moment. By letting go of the past, we make room for miracles to replace our grievances."

At first, I doubted the truth of this, at least as it pertained to me, especially because at this point, I really didn't feel as though I had anyone to forgive. On the other hand, I couldn't deny that I always seemed to be in a holding pattern, taking two steps forward and one step back. Eventually, though I didn't believe forgiveness could have this much power over my life, I decided to come up with some names and offer forgiveness to anyone I could think of who had done me wrong. What did I have to lose?

As I began to make the list, I was amazed at how many childhood hurts I was still holding onto; in some cases, I couldn't even remember the name of the person, just the incident. I had to forgive my parents for letting my second-grade teacher pass me to the next grade, even though we all discussed that I shouldn't move onto the next grade level unless I went to summer school, which I didn't. After that I always fell behind the other students, which caused me a lot of stress and embarrassment.

In middle school, I started dating my first boyfriend, only to have him drop me like a hot potato. This crushed my ego and self-worth tremendously! To make matters worse, he had an ex-girlfriend who was in a gang and now wanted to fight me because I had taken him away from her. She and her friends continued to bully me for a year, to the point that I considered taking my own life. I hadn't thought about them in years, but now, as I added them to my forgiveness list, I realized I had still been unknowingly carrying the weight of what they had done to me.

These are just a few examples from a list that took an hour to complete and wound up filling an entire piece of paper, not including the stuff I had to forgive MYSELF for! When I was finished with this process, I noticed that I felt better in a lighter, brighter way, as if I had set down a heavy bag. I now do this process every January and have found it's a wonderful way to start the year off.

The Forgiveness Process TOOL

First, PLUG IN and ask that who you need to forgive will be revealed through this process. Then write down everyone and anyone you can think of who has done you wrong or didn't have your best interest in mind. If you don't know or remember their names, you can put down the memory of what they did. When you're done, tear the paper up, throw it away, or burn it—whatever feels right to you. Then say the following FORGIVENESS AFFIRMATION: "I bless you; I send you love and forgiveness, and I now set you free. You no longer have a hold on me. I NOW claim the healthy life and (*insert miracle here*) that I deserve!"

Repeat this affirmation whenever you think of that person or situation. You'll find your intention to set them free sets you free as well. It really is that simple, I promise you.

After doing this process, pay special attention to your Inner Guidance. For example, if someone mentions a counselor that really helped them or you keep hearing the same advertisement for a therapist, or you suddenly see a support group specializing in an issue you want to overcome, ask yourself, "Is this MY NEXT BEST STEP to my healing or miracles?" Notice what you feel and see. Does it feel good to reach out to that therapist, or does it feel heavy? Does it seem bright and light to go to that support group? If this NEXT STEP is from your Inner Guidance, it is also most likely the accelerant or silver bullet that will help all the other tools in this book fall into place.

The weak can never forgive.
Forgiveness is the attribute of the strong.
—Mahatma Gandhi

WEEK FIVE ACTIVATION STEPS:
THE EXPERIMENT PARTY

(Combines the whole chapter in the following steps.)

Now it's time to put the exercise from the beginning of this chapter into practice. Just follow the directions below. *(The following three things are for you as the host to do before the actual experiment.)*

Invite Your Friends, Family or Team

- You will need at least three other people to conduct this experiment, but more is even better! Be sure to have a space (i.e. a family or dining room) big enough for all the guests to sit while you stand in front and guide them through the experiment.

Explain to your invitees that you just read about this fun experiment in an amazing book and you want them to participate so they can experience the results firsthand.

- Other than the directions, don't give them any details. You don't want their conscious mind deciding the results before the experiment is complete. *(Of course, if you are meeting with your MIRACLE TEAM they already know what to expect, which is fine. While others may decide from the start that they don't believe in the experiment, thus creating a self-fulfilling prophecy, team members are also reading this book and seeking to transform their negative beliefs, therefore, they are far less likely to try to discredit, dismiss it, or taint it.)*

- Choose something for your participant to read during the experiment. Make sure it is something neutral, that evokes neither negative nor strong positive feelings, as this could affect the results. I prefer the local events or entertainment section of a newspaper.
- Ask for two volunteers, one to serve as the "participant" and one to record the comments of the participant and the "audience." If nobody or everyone volunteers, choose the person who has the best "go with the flow" personality" as the participant and the most meticulous person for the note-taking.
- Have the participant come up and stand beside you, then hand them the reading material and ask him or her to silently read it. They are to think of nothing else while they read it. (Make sure they are standing for the whole exercise, both times!)

First ACTION STEP: Read the Following to the Guests:

"You are not going to like what I'm going to ask you to do, but in order for this exercise to work you need to follow my directions exactly.

"Now, look at (fill in the participant's name) reading the newspaper and for the next minute consciously think negative thoughts about her/him, for example, "I hate her shoes" or "That is an ugly dress," or whatever you can come up with. You do not need to believe these things; you can just pretend you mean it. The alarm will ring when one minute is up."

Now, start the timer for one minute.

Second ACTION STEP:

When the bell rings, tell your participant they can stop reading but need to stay standing in front of the room with you.

- Confirm that your note-taker is ready to write down everyone's comments.
- Address each audience member individually, asking them to describe their experience during that one minute. Then turn to your participant and ask what his/her experience was.

Third ACTION STEP:

- Now excuse yourself and the participant and go into another room where the others cannot hear what you are going to say. Give him or her the following instructions:

  "We are going to do the exercise for another minute, but this time you and I are going to send or INTEND good feelings and/or love to the audience. Imagine a beautiful light surrounding them with health, happiness, love or ANY OTHER POSITIVE THING you can think of, and/or things you appreciate about them, *even if you don't know them or mean it!* (Suggest to the participant that he/she close either their eyes or look above the guests' heads while sending them good thoughts, as making eye contact with them is distracting. Also, it is more powerful this way!)

- Return to the main room and tell your guests that they are to follow the same directions as they did during the first minute (re-read the directions if needed).

Start the timer for one minute.

Fourth ACTION STEP:

- Stop when the timer alerts you.
- Ask the guests what they noticed this time and if there was anything different from the first minute.
- Ask the participant what he/she noticed this time and if anything was different for them during the second minute.
- Read the following out loud: "This experiment is now complete. I'm going to read you a summary of what typically happens during this experiment, then we'll compare this group's responses. After we read through the results, I will explain what this experiment is supposed to demonstrate."
- **Read the typical responses from the audience for the FIRST minute.**
  - o "I was uncomfortable!"
  - o "I felt horrible!"
  - o "It was the longest minute of my life!"
  - o "I had a hard time thinking of negative thoughts!"
- **Read the typical responses from the participant for the FIRST minute.**
  - o "I couldn't concentrate to read!"
  - o "My thoughts felt foggy!"
  - o "I had a hard time standing, I felt like I was being pushed backwards!"

(Be sure to tell the audience that every participant has some sort of physical experience during the exercise, and that the audience typically comments that they noticed the participant swinging back and forth, as if they were dizzy or could just not stand still.)

- **Read the typical responses from the audience for the SECOND minute.**
  - "This time was even harder to do than the minute before!"
  - "I couldn't concentrate!"
  - "I had a hard time thinking of things to be negative about!"
  - "This time felt longer than the first minute!"
- **Read the typical responses from the participant for the SECOND minute.**
  - "I felt stronger and had no problem standing!"
  - "I felt good!"
  - "The time went by fast!"
- **Review the responses from the current experiment and compare them to the typical responses.**
- Tell the audience that the only difference between the first and second minutes was that during the second minute you and the participant sent them positive thoughts or INTENDED good feelings, and imagined a beautiful light surrounding them with health, happiness, love or any other positive things you could think of, and/or things you appreciated about them *even if you didn't know them personally or mean it!*
- **Summarize and explain the experiment.**
  "This experiment was a fun way to understand how powerful your thoughts are, even when you do not mean what you are thinking! Your thoughts really do affect you and those around you! If you enjoyed this, please consider creating your own book club and learning more about using your thoughts to positively transform your life and the world around you, one person at a time!"

*NOTE: If an audience member found it was easier to have negative thoughts during the second minute, it may mean that this person is not producing their own energy and is unconsciously attaching energetically to other people in order to feel good or receive more energy. Why do I say this? Because when someone is being negative and positivity is blasted their way, that positive energy should "neutralize" the negative person, who will then lose the ability to concentrate on the negative issue or lose interest in being negative toward the POSITIVE SENDER. However, when a person becomes more energized with NEGATIVITY when positive energy is sent their way, this is a sign that they are not regularly connecting to their Higher Source for inner guidance, consistent wellbeing and energy, thereby creating an ENER-GETIC feast or famine cycle. Imagine you hadn't eaten for days and then all of a sudden people start throwing food at you. You would probably continue to devour the food even after you're full because you're not sure when you're going to see food again and feeling like you're starving is so horrible that you're going to take whatever you can get in the hopes it will fill you up until next time. This can be the case with energy as well.

To find out if this applies to you, ask yourself this question: have you ever visited with someone for an hour or so and when it was time for you to go your separate ways the other person mentioned how tired they are, or said they needed coffee? Or do they simply look more tired or worn out than they did in the beginning of your meeting?

And what about your energy level? If you feel full of energy, more positive than before or as if you drank a whole bunch of coffee, you may be unconsciously taking other people's positive energy.

Also, ask those close to you if they have ever noticed feeling tired or drained after meeting with you. If the answer is yes, continue or consider reading this book because it will teach you how to PLUG IN to YOUR OWN SOURCE OF ENERGY. This way, you will no longer absorb others' energy and they won't easily be able to take yours.

I send POSITIVE
Thoughts and

GOOD *Intentions*

everywhere I go.
Any negativity sent
my way is
Neutralized

IMMEDIATELY!

✂

Say the following affirming mantra whenever somebody really bothers you and you're having a hard time NOT THINKING ABOUT THEM or THE SITUATION and you are ready to be FREE of this person or problem. Essentially, you're releasing it to your Higher Power for a miraculous solution!

I *Bless* you,

I send you *Love*

(or good intentions)

and

I AM NOW SET *Free!*

Chapter 6

Give Them Something to Talk About

ow you will throw caution to the wind, The Universe and everyone around you, because you ACCEPT and EXPECT that what you are wanting is a DONE DEAL! The NEW YOU has begun the transformation from the inside out and you no longer relate to the old issues—sickness, depression, loneliness, or whatever made you feel sorry for yourself—that made you the person you were yesterday. Today, you will learn the tools that creates DEEP and PROFOUND changes, both consciously and unconsciously, that you will communicate to yourself and to the world. They will be a daily reminder that you are not the same old person and you'll no longer accept your old ways of being!

A New You for a New Day TOOL

Start your morning differently than you did as the OLD YOU; this way, each day is a reminder that your life is changing and improving. Maybe set your alarm fifteen or more minutes earlier so you're not rushed and you can begin your day with one or more of the following: meditation, yoga, reading the Bible, exercising, journaling, prayer, or using guidance cards. I personally look forward to thirty extra minutes of quiet time in the morning after

I have PLUGGED IN. I do the following:

- A healthy protein drink packed with one or more of the following; fruits, vegetables, flavorless powder bone broth, and collagen.
- An affirmation or oracle card reading so that my Higher Power, Angels, and Guides can give me input and inspiration about my day. This way I have actual visual reminders that I am not alone and that I am guided easily and effortlessly to accomplish all my goals and my to-do list.
- A releasement prayer for anything I feel anxious or overwhelmed with that day.

This has become a very special time for me because I'm starting my day by feeding my body and soul the healthy nutrition it needs. It is also during this time that my Higher Power, my mind, body, and soul talk to me, and when I often hear what my NEXT BEST STEP is for that day.

Continue Your Day with Newness

- Try to make different choices all day long! Consider driving a different route to work or when doing your errands; take a webinar class for a new hobby at lunchtime. Go to new places that you have never been for groceries, shopping, restaurants, et cetera. Consider eating food you have never tried before.
- In the evening, take a new route home from work. Cook a dinner you have never made before, then unwind after work with a new activity (i.e. if you normally watch TV, listen instead to podcasts or an audiobook; take an online workshop that introduces you to different ideas; put together a puzzle; take a hot bath with a glass of wine, et

cetera. (THIS ALSO MAY BE AN IDEAL TIME TO DO THE WEEKLY HOMEWORK FROM THIS BOOK!)

Create Unconscious Reminders TOOL

One of my favorite ways to utilize this tool is to change all of my account passwords to positive affirmations. This is actually a two-for-one tool; you make the changes on a conscious level, then affirm them unconsciously each time you use the positive passwords to log into your accounts.

These kinds of little, new choices become self-fulfilling prophecies; they begin the process of you feeling and believing that you are actively changing—mind, body and soul.

Sample Passwords:

- Sexy healthy (your name)
- Money magnet (your name)
- I am a miracle mama (or man)
- True love found me (include the year)
- I am now healthy & wealthy
- I am NOW happily ever after

Why These Changes Work

Science has proven that incorporating new actions and thoughts into your routine *literally* creates a new you. This is because doing new things stimulates parts of your brain that you are not currently using, thereby creating new neural pathways, new habits, and eventually, a new life. Think of it as forging a hiking trail to a secret oasis you found. In the beginning, as you travel to the oasis, you would need to pay very close attention to where you are and where you are going so that you don't get lost. Eventually, though, the hiking trail will become so familiar that you can get to your oasis without thinking of every step you take. The same is true when creating a route to the new you. You need only believe enough to take the first steps, then trust that your Higher Power, and the new pathways in your brain, will continue to guide you.

Make CONSCIOUS CHOICES that will become UNCONSCIOUS REMINDERS of the TRANSFORMED LIFE you are believing to receive.

Give Them Something to Talk About TOOL

Now is also the ideal time to make those external changes you've perhaps been wanting to do but never had the confidence or motivation. Get a new haircut and/or color, buy new clothes that are a different style from what you normally wear, and/or choose a different shade of lipstick. If you're a guy, maybe grow or shave off a beard. These changes, even small ones, are not just skin deep. They announce, every time you look in the mirror or when you run into family or friends, that you are no longer the same person. Don't be surprised if people start saying, "Something is different about you," even if they can't quite put their finger on what it is. This is a wonderful reminder to you that you are in the process of evolving and activating the miracles in your life.

Excuses Keep Us STUCK and MISERABLE

One of the things I loved most about being a hairstylist was that I got to help women and men make those positive changes. I knew that changing their image was often a catalyst for the deep inner changes they desired in their lives. I would often make suggestions for a new look, especially when a client was feeling stuck in a certain area of her life, was going through a bad breakup or divorce, had a job they hated or was just down in the dumps. Roughly half of these women and men would take me up on these suggestions and remark, before I was even done with their hair, "I already feel better!"

The other half, however, declined to make any sort of change; they also inevitably had a whole bunch of well-practiced excuses as to why. I would often hear things like, "No Bernadette, I don't think I should change my hair until I lose my weight," or "When (fill in the blank) happens in my life, then I'll make those changes."

I was always amazed by how many women told me they wouldn't or couldn't make any changes to their appearance because they weren't currently where they wanted to be. When I probed a little further, I often found an underlying sense of unworthiness, such as, "I don't deserve it yet," or "I don't want to waste money on myself when I am this size! When I am the weight I want to be I will buy a whole new closetful of clothes."

They also had several ways of dealing with not liking themselves, all of which involved ignoring their extra weight rather than changing it. These included:

- "I don't own a full-length mirror."
- "I don't look at myself after I leave the house."
- "I hate shopping or trying on clothes. I only buy clothes online because of the low price, elastic band and easy sizing of LG, XL, XXL."

If you find that you can relate to this, I would ask you this question: "How motivated are you to make changes when your whole world revolves around avoiding what you do not like in your life?" The answer is, *not motivated at all!* While in this mindset it is much easier to avoid looking in the mirror and going to clothing stores, and to accept hating your body and being miserable! Then, when you're having a "bad day," it's too quick and easy to go through a drive-thru and get another three-hundred-calorie latte and, though you might feel a little guilty, you tell yourself you deserve a little pick-me-up, because OFTEN IT'S THE ONLY GIFT YOU GIVE YOURSELF. This has become the acceptable status quo for far too many people!

Some people actually believe self-loathing is a powerful motivator. "One of these days," a woman said to me, "I'll hate how I look so much, that will motivate me to finally lose weight!"

This is completely contrary to my experience of working with countless women and men over the past two decades. I found when you want things to drastically and rapidly change in your life, it is best to start with the simple things I mentioned above. They act as a magical accelerant for attracting positive, long-lasting, life-transforming experiences like losing the weight, finding the ideal career and attracting the ideal mate.

How I Lied to Myself for Fifteen Years

My experience with excuses is not just professional, but personal. In fact, before embarking on my outer transformational journey I had spent twenty years brainwashing myself into not making changes, because I decided I couldn't!

This changed on my fortieth birthday, when my husband took me to the Bahamas to swim with the dolphins. It had been my dream vacation for as long as I could remember, and as I lay on the beach that first day, sipping a margarita and soaking in the sun,

I truly felt like I was in heaven. It was while I was in this relaxed, almost meditative state, that I asked the Universe to reveal to me the best changes I could make in this fortieth year of my life. Instantly, I saw myself in my mind's eye with short hair above my shoulders. The vision brought a huge smile to my face and a feeling of pure bliss and happiness. This was rather surprising to me, as my hair had reached the middle of my back since I was in my twenties. I loved it this way and had never considered a change, but now I found myself very excited about the possibility. A second later I was snapped out of my bliss by the thought, *You can't make changes to your hair. It's too kinky and curly when it's short!* The negative thought in the midst of such bliss was a jolt. I sat up on my beach chair and without even thinking, I said out loud, "Bernadette, you are a *hairstylist*! You straighten people's hair for a living! You can do anything you want to your own *effing* hair!"

Believing I couldn't have shorter hair was the lie I had been telling myself, because in actuality my hair had been more wavy than curly ever since the birth of my son fifteen years earlier. But in my mind it hadn't changed, and my belief, based on old programming, was so strong that it was affecting how I saw myself. The power of the mind is really quite amazing.

This realization was a huge one for me, and a confirmation that this was going to be my year of many changes. After that I could barely wait to get back home to get my hair cut. I couldn't wait to meet the NEW ME!

Once I embraced this simple but drastic life change, I didn't look back. In fact, I loved it. Sure, it was a bit jarring at first. I'd catch myself in the mirror and would be surprised by the woman with short, straight hair looking back at me. But then I would say to myself, "Oh, I forgot, this is the NEW ME. That boring old me is gone and I'm NOW sassy and sexy!"

There was just something about walking and feeling my hair

bounce that made me feel ready to take on the world and any new endeavors. Shortly thereafter I decided to retire as a hairstylist and follow my dream career as an author and life-changing transformational coach.

WEEK SIX ACTIVATION STEP:
Invest In YOURSELF

If you don't invest in yourself, neither will The Universe or anybody else for that matter. I have found this is to be especially true when it comes to women and their romantic relationships. More often than not, if a woman is not spending money and time on herself the man in her life won't feel the need to spend very much money or time on her either. In most cases this is not done purposefully, it is simply the Universal Law of Attraction in action. According to this law, "like attracts like"; this means your mate, your boss, your friends, and The Universe act like energetic mirrors, reflecting back to you what is ACCEPTED and/or EXPECTED IN YOUR WORLD!

Remember in the beginning of this chapter we declared it was time to start throwing caution to the wind, announcing to yourself and the world that you are not the same old person you were yesterday. Today, you begin to invest in yourself and your future with the following ACTION STEPS. Be sure to share with your Miracle Team each "investment step" you are taking so you can hold each other accountable for making those changes throughout the week. Before making *any* decision be sure to PLUG IN and ask for Inner Guidance to see if it is truly your NEXT BEST STEP. Announce these positive changes to people you know and, if appropriate, on Facebook or other social media outlets. Because this is your announcement physically and energetically to everyone, "Watch out world I'm UPLEVELING, and I now expect other major changes, miracles and manifestations in every area of my life! I will no longer accept the old mediocre me!" Whatever you do, make sure to have fun with it!

First ACTION STEP: Invest TIME in Yourself

According to the Nielson Media Research Company, the typical American watched an average of eight hours and fifty-five minutes of TV per day in 2018. We should all consider that statistic the next time we say we don't have time to work on improving ourselves!

- Begin with scheduling "YOU TIME" in your day planner. This is the gift you give yourself—your alone time that belongs to you and nobody else. This is an unspoken statement to the Universe that creates a precedence of YOUR VALUE. Since you are your first priority every day, others will also unconsciously emulate you as a priority.

- Start by setting set your alarm (do it RIGHT NOW!) for fifteen minutes earlier than you normally get up. Spend those fifteen minutes doing something to feed your body and soul. You might start by eating something healthy, then choose an activity (i.e. yoga, meditation, journaling) that you want to do. Don't feel obligated to stick with just one thing; try whatever you feel guided to and alternate as much as you like. I suggest starting out with a week, but I'm willing to bet you will enjoy those fifteen minutes so much they will soon become part of regular NEW YOU routine.

- Change at least two passwords that you use every day to a positive statement that you want to be true. This way, you will be consciously affirming your miracles to your subconscious every time you log into an account!

- For the rest of the week, try changing up your morning routine, whether it's taking a different route to work or eating something new for breakfast, et cetera.

Second ACTION STEP: Invest MONEY in Yourself

- Spend money on something for yourself that you normally wouldn't. Remember, this is especially important if you're working on your abundance. This does not have to be an extreme amount of money. Even two dollars on something you consider frivolous, like your favorite candy bar, can make you feel good and create a positive reaction in the Universe that comes back to you in unexpected ways.

- This week, change one thing about your physical appearance that will act as a statement to your family, friends and the world that you are not the same old person they knew yesterday! To get this energetic ball rolling, decide NOW what you will change or upgrade. Will it be a new haircut, color or style? If so, then take the ACTION STEP and schedule it NOW! Or, will you go shopping and get a few new items of clothing that are a different style from what the old you would have chosen (i.e. something more professional, elegant, sassy or fun)?

- During the day, try something different for lunch. Perhaps eat something that seems extravagant to you or go to a restaurant that makes you feel abundant while being there. Even if you only have coffee and dessert, enjoy the atmosphere and saver the food with each bite, using all of your senses while envisioning yourself there in the future having a complete meal with no worries about the cost!

Insider Beauty Secret

These changes do not have to be expensive! If you're wanting a complete makeover but it doesn't fit in the budget right now, consider going to a beauty school and getting a stylist that is just about ready to graduate. Here is the secret that most people don't know: a stylist about to graduate has already passed most of their tests and is just finishing some loose ends while they prepare for their final certification requirements. In my opinion, you're more likely to be pampered at a beauty school, because the cosmetologists, makeup artists, aestheticians, and manicurists take their time to make sure they do everything right and "by the book." This means you'll get really fabulous massages during your facials, manicures and pedicures, and head shampoos because each technician is taught about all the pressure points from head to toe to help clients have the most relaxing experience. They also don't skip steps because the teacher could be watching them and, in any event, will ask the client about the quality of the service they received. This is not the case once technicians get out into the real-world salons, when they don't always have time to concentrate on those little things that make getting such services so wonderful.

Hints from a Fashion Junkie on a Budget

For current fashions at a good price consider going to discount stores like TJ Maxx, Ross, Burlington Coat Factory, Nordstrom Rack, et cetera, both online and in person. I have found some of my favorite items at these types of stores; however, I've met a lot of clients who hate to go to them because they get so overwhelmed by so many choices. Let me share with you some little tricks of the trade I have learned as a fashion junkie.

- **When you are shopping for items at a jam-packed discount store, have (at least) a general idea of what you are looking for before you arrive.** For example, rather than thinking, "I want five new outfits," which is very vague, it would be easier to break it down into "two pairs of dress pants, two dress shirts and three new business dresses." Otherwise, you'll get lost, scattered, confused and exhausted before you find anything you are looking for.

- **Only go to the select areas of the store that pertain to your shopping list.** If you need a new shirt to create your transformed look (i.e. that of a prosperous business-woman), only look in the areas of the store with professional looking shirts in your size. This shouldn't be difficult, as these stores typically group items by style and size; for example, all the sweaters are together, all the coats are together, and so on.

- **Only look at the colors that are best for your skin tone and hair color.** Because looking at every single shirt in your size will exhaust you and drive you crazy!

- **Don't forget to look at the purses and shoes that will add that finished, polished touch to your upgraded look!** I have personally found that these items affect my abundance mindset immediately, especially if I'm working on more prosperity in my life. This is because throughout the day I see them more than anything else I'm wearing, so they're a constant reminder that, "OH YES, I'm worth investing in! That is why I have these beautiful shoes on and this fabulous purse." For this reason, I suggest spending a little more money on these two items, and I promise you will not regret it.

Why Consignment or Thrift Stores are Not My First Suggestion:

I do not have anything against these kinds of stores because they often have good options; however, they are not my first choice when I'm trying to UPLEVEL my self-worth or abundance mindset. I find that brand-new items, regardless of cost, more clearly represent, "I am truly investing in myself" and thus make that energetic transition a little smoother and faster for me. That said, no matter where you choose to go shopping, ALWAYS PLUG IN to your Higher Power and use your own Inner Guidance as to whether something feels light, dark or heavy. This will guide you as you decide what your Next Best Step is as you UPLEVEL YOUR LIFE mentally, physically and spiritually!

"Investing in yourself is the best investment you will ever make. It will not only improve your life; it will improve the lives of all those around you."

—Robin Sharma

Third ACTION STEP: Invest ENERGY in Yourself

Earlier I mentioned that we have more time than we think we do; it's all a matter of reorganizing it to make room for new activities and habits. The same is true for our energy; in our busy lives it's easy to feel overwhelmed and like we don't have the mental or physical energy to do something outside our normal routine, but this is only the case if you believe it to be so! This week, after work, you're going to invest your energy in something you want to have accomplished in the near future. This can be developing a new skill, a new hobby, or a new career, or it can be something fun you haven't done in years. It can be anything that lights you up from the inside out! When you spend time and energy doing the things that make your soul shine, the light attracts more good to you and gives you energy to do the mundane everyday things that need to be done. Below are some suggestions that I've noticed have made the biggest positive changes for my clients.

- Take online classes for the degree you always wanted.
- Watch webinars and videos that teach you a new skill or a hobby.
- Call or go see that friend or family member you haven't had time to talk to.
- Begin writing that book you've always dreamed about writing.
- Take a short walk.
- Learn to meditate or do yoga.

NOTE: My experience of helping people reinvent themselves for 20+ years, is that other people generally like to see you the way they've always seen you because it's more comfortable for them. Don't worry, they will get comfortable with the new you soon! This may take approximately 30 days, especially for your mate or others that are close to you. That's okay because physical and mental changes must be made to activate your miracles. Please post your before-and-after pictures on our Believe It to Receive IT Facebook page.

I KNOW
I AM
Worth it

SO
I EASILY INVEST
in *Myself!*

✂

I feel *Worth* a

MILLION BUCKS

or *More*

and

it *Shows!*

✂

Chapter 7
Love It or Let It Go

 $\mathcal{T}$ his is one of the most life-changing chapters of this book. This will be your go-to chapter whenever you feel your Higher Power or The Universe is not moving fast enough for you, or when you feel stuck mentally, physically or spiritually and don't know what your Next Best Step is to transform your life and create miracles.

What follows is the fastest way to STOP any conscious or unconscious self-sabotaging, energy- blocking routines that could be affecting or postponing your hopes, dreams and prayers from getting answered.

You will be moving items, a physical action that also serves to move your own stuck energy. When you combine this action with mentally working on issues in your life (i.e. using the tools in the other chapters in this book), the results are dramatic. Think of it as an energetic "Big Bang," creating a new environment for your transformed life to appear!

This exercise is rooted in the concept that everything is made up of energy, even inanimate objects. Take a rock, for example. Though to the naked eye it appears inert, on a molecular level it is made of energy, and if you were to look at it under a very powerful microscope you would see those molecules moving.

People who are highly sensitive can feel the difference between one rock and another, or one person's house and another. Even if you're not aware of energy on a conscious level, you may have said at one time or another, "I don't feel good whenever I go into that office building." Or, "I feel so good, sitting in your favorite chair looking at your garden!" Unconsciously, you may be picking up on the energy—positive or negative—of the building, or of the people who work there, and even "Mother Nature's energy." Later in this chapter we will discuss the conscious and unconscious factors that contribute to these different sensations and experiences.

The purpose of this chapter is to raise your conscious awareness of how the things you choose to surround yourself with are affecting you positively or negatively, whether you are aware of it or not. This is often why you may have unexplainable good days or lucky moments or unexplained tiredness, sadness, blah feeling, lack of hope, or a stuck feeling.

What It Looks Like in Real Life

As we've discussed throughout this book, our current reality is a reflection of our beliefs and expectations to that point, but when our current reality is not reflecting what we want, it's very hard to believe in even the possibility that things can be different. To break this cycle and transform your life ASAP into the life that you desire, you must improve or change the underlying conscious, unconscious and subconscious communication you are receiving and interpreting from the world around you. You must make the choice to truly love and appreciate everything and everyone in your day-to-day surroundings, without any bad feelings or memories attached to them. Most importantly, the items that surround you cannot be extreme opposites of everything you're hoping, dreaming of or praying for—in other words, the Transformed Life you designed back in Chapter 3.

Let's say, for example, that your IDEAL LIFE is being happily married, rich and healthy. Your spouse in this ideal life is your true soulmate who values you and your relationship. Being married to this person would also double your household income, which makes for a very comfortable standard of living.

Now let's imagine if this was your current reality. The first thing you see when you wake up each morning is the picture of you and your ex-husband on your wedding day. You tell yourself that you only keep it for the kids (you have two of them, which you're now raising on your own), so they can maintain a sense of normalcy. The truth is, every time you see it you are uncomfortable because it reminds you that your marriage failed and that you are single and lonely.

Next, you get out of bed to take a shower. As you are drying yourself off you notice your towel is worn out and faded, with two small holes. You tell yourself, "That's okay, because nobody sees this towel but me. I keep the 'good set' folded in the closet for when I have guests (which in reality is maybe once a year)." Then you remind yourself, "The kids don't even notice all the bleach stains on their towels, so neither should I."

Then you go into the kitchen to make breakfast, using the cooking set that you received as a wedding gift from your ex in-laws, another unconscious reminder that you are currently not married. When you and the kids are ready to leave the house (which you and your ex chose together—another unconscious negative reminder that you're now single and alone), you get in your car and notice the crack in your windshield, just another reminder that you are living paycheck to paycheck and do not have money to fix it. You don't think about the windshield for long, though, because you soon drive past your doctor's office, which reminds you that you still owe them money for your emergency visit two months ago and if you don't make a payment soon they will send you to collections, AGAIN. Finally, you get the kids to school, give them a hug and kiss and tell them their father will pick them up at the end of the day, because it is "his weekend."

As you say those words you feel your heart break just a little more and your stomach drops because this means you will be spending another Saturday and Sunday all alone.

How REAL LIFE is Sabotaging Your IDEAL LIFE

In the above example, you are literally surrounded by reminders that your current reality is not what you are wanting. It does not matter whether you concentrate on or *just scan* the wedding picture, cooking set, the house you live in, the cracked windshield or the doctor's office—your brain is still registering, unconsciously and subconsciously, your past memories, symbolic meanings and current feelings of failure and lack, not to mention triggering your future fears of loneliness! In other words, these items (or your perception of them) are sabotaging the activation of your ideal life, ALL day ALL the time!

It doesn't matter that you're really good at keeping these feelings in check and hidden from everybody else, and perhaps even yourself. The truth is, you are consciously reminding yourself of past failures and of your present lack of abundance, and on an unconscious level you have surrounded yourself with things that remind you of exactly what you do not want to be true in your life. You will not be receiving any "Best Actor Award," but what you will receive is a whole lot more of what you already have.

When you want to CHANGE what your life looks like to the world, the only thing that matters are WHAT'S GOING ON IN YOUR INNER WORLD.

How are you CURRENTLY THINKING, FEELING and BELIEVING?

Because your INNER WORLD BELIEFS determine what is possible for your FUTURE WORLD!"

The previous scenario included examples of possible triggers and how they unconsciously register in your mind and body—and that was just during the first two hours of the day! Now imagine other negative reminders triggering you throughout the workday and evening, all the way up until bedtime, and how this might be keeping you from activating miracles in your life.

Work Example

Perhaps you feel unappreciated and underpaid, which may be reflected in your workspace; for example, you don't have the extra money to add personal items, or you wish you had a perfect family picture to put on your desk but currently you don't have a family. Because of this, whenever you look at your desk where you believe that picture should be, or at the walls and see how sparsely decorated they are, you are reminded, all day long, of everything you wish you had.

The typical person spends about eight hours, five days a week, working away from home; this means your workspace is one of the most important areas of influence in your life. It also speaks about you to all others who enter it. It tells them who you are, how prosperous you are or are not, and what standards are acceptable to you. It even serves as a first impression for those you've never met before. Ask yourself, "What does my office say about me to others when they enter the room or sit in here for a meeting?" This can be a very profound realization, especially if you have been passed over for promotions or are stuck in a career you hate.

This Chapter's ONLY TOOL: BEWARE of Self-Sabotage

Remember, the purpose of this chapter is to learn how to accelerate our transformation when we feel stuck or that things are moving too slowly. To do this, we must also have an understanding of how the things that surround us energetically effect our daily lives and often sabotages our ability to activate the miracles we are wanting. The only tool for this chapter is to help you to become aware of the different cloaks self-sabotage wears; this way, when you're in the process of reevaluating your life you will be able to see everything, including the things that surround you, with a new perspective. You'll be able to clearly discern whether you LOVE IT or if it's time to LET IT GO.

As seen in the previous examples, if you want to transform and re-create your life into the one you've dreamed and prayed about, it is imperative that you make positive changes in your physical surroundings. This way, you knowingly incorporate and acknowledge in your everyday life that profound mantra: "That was the old me, this is the NEW ME!" NOT changing your environment is an example of the most insidious type of self-sabotage—consciously, unconsciously and subconsciously. Don't worry, though, I'm not going to make you move or do anything you don't want to do. However, I will give you some examples of how we disguise self-sabotage in our life.

What I have heard from my students:

The number one thing I hear at my workshops is, "This chapter does not apply to me." If this thought occurs to you, let this be a RED FLAG because this chapter is for everybody, especially those who think it is not for them!

I have heard every kind of reason for why people don't need to do this, including,

- "I just took stuff to the Salvation Army last week, last month or last year."
- "My partner is a hoarder and this could cause problems in our relationship."
- "I don't have extra things."
- "I already Love EVERYTHING that surrounds me."

I could list examples forever; the point is for you to understand that your OLD way of thinking and doing things has created the situation you are currently in. So if you TRULY WANT YOUR TRANSFORMED LIFE YOU'RE GOING TO NEED TO DO SOME WORK on the things that surround you!

When you do the following steps, you will immediately start to bring into your life MORE OF WHAT YOU WANT, as you RELEASE THE THINGS IN YOUR LIFE THAT REPRESENT WHAT YOU DO NOT WANT!

"For it is in GIVING that we RECEIVE."

—St. Francis of Assisi

WEEK SEVEN ACTIVATION STEPS:
ALIGNING with the FUTURE You WANT

This tool essentially requires you to DETOX and CLEAR THE ENERGY that surrounds you while you clean and rearrange your home with a new and different perspective, that being getting rid of anything that is not aligned with Your Transformed Ideal Life. As stated above, don't worry. This doesn't mean you have to throw out everything you own, for example, if you are currently living in poverty and your dream is to be rich one day. It is really about asking yourself if you LOVE the things that surround you AND if those things ONLY remind you of positive experiences. IF NOT, LET IT GO!

Be Mindful

Through this whole process PLUG IN and use your Inner Guidance and the tools you learned in Chapter 1. When you're not sure about an item put it in your hand and ask yourself, "Does this feel dark or heavy, or does it look or seem bright or dull?"

Choosing Your "Miracle Room"

I suggest that at this time you choose *one* room to concentrate on that correlates with the area of your life you're currently focused most on transforming. For example, if you are focused on your love life, choose your bedroom; if you're working on your health, choose the kitchen; and if you're working on your prosperity and abundance choose your office or work area. (Remember, you have all week to do the following steps, so if you're able to do more than one room, then by all means, go for it!)

Be sure to share this process with your Miracle Team to keep you accountable, and consider taking before and after pictures to share with them and/or on the *"Believe IT to Receive IT"* closed Facebook page. Be aware that others, even some of your team members, may have real resistance towards this chapter, and if so, acknowledge this and release it to your Higher Power to deal with. Your job is to help each other focus ONLY on the END RESULT, that being an energetically cleansed living area and life that helps create the right space for miracles.

First ACTION STEP: What Love Is Not

- Focus on anything you have not used in the last year because this means you are NOT LOVING IT!
- Next, take a look at things that do not have a good memory attached to them.
- Now, look at anything that is NOT energetically in alignment with the Transformed Life you want to create!

For example, if your dream is to be financially abundant, you are looking for anything that makes you feel poor, especially items that are not good enough to donate because they are so used and abused. I once saw an interview with a Catholic priest who was accepting clothes and household donations for a homeless shelter. *"Please,"* he said, *"do not bring any items that have holes in them or are really worn, because we're trying to help the homeless keep their dignity and self-worth during this challenging time in their lives."* I think about what that priest said every time I go through my old items. If it is not good enough for homeless people, then it is not good enough for me (or you) anymore either.

Creating Space for Your Miracles

As you do this, think about the transformed life you want to be represented in the room you are working on this week. If your dream is to attract a romantic soulmate, then as you go through your bedroom now be sure to make room for this person, for example, creating space in your closet for them to hang their clothes. Do the same as you move through the rest of the house, creating space for them and their items in your bathroom and kitchen. Get rid of that plaque that says, "#1 Bachelor," or anything that confirms you are single or claims something opposite of what you truly want for your NEW MIRACULOUS LIFE!

Healthier Choices

If you are wanting to be at a healthier weight, go through your kitchen, get rid of all the junk food, and stock up on healthy food. If your family is not supportive of your new food choices, don't worry, because there are workarounds. For example, I do a cleanse and detox diet once or twice a year and my family does not. I find it helpful when I can ONLY see my healthy food choices when I'm hungry, so I create my own separate shelf in a cupboard and the fridge. I also tell my family I will not be going down the junk food aisles when I'm shopping because the cookies, soda pop and pastries are just too hard for me to resist. They will need to go to the store for those items themselves. Then I make it a point to put the junk food they buy in the pantry, not on the countertop, so it is "out of sight, out of mind." I simply refuse to consciously allow sabotage as I choose to become healthier!

How to Simplify the Clearing Process

I suggest you begin the above steps with a fast, general sweep through the chosen room or living area. Grab the items you have not used in one year and that you do not have good memories about or things that do not create that loving feeling. Anything that is in plain sight, don't think twice about, or worry that you may not have anything to replace it with (yet!). I will cover that later in this chapter.

This is the time to get energy moving in these areas of your life, ASAP! Take these items and put them in a space or a room that is not used much (I personally use my dining room area since my family and I only eat formal dinners a couple of times a year). Whatever area you choose, make sure it's one you can still get to if need be, but secluded enough that the items will be out of sight and out of mind.

Second ACTION STEP: Dig Deep for Stuck Energy

Drawers

Go through these areas by taking out every item, then vacuuming or wiping all crumbs, dirt and dust out. Look for anything that doesn't have a clear purpose or has missing parts. I throw most of those items away without hesitation, but once in a while I feel like something may be important to my family members. I put these items in a box and ask them if there's anything in there they want to keep, or if they know where the missing part is. Most of the time my family doesn't even care enough to look in the box before I throw the items away. One time I found twenty extra keys—for what, nobody knew! I threw them away and created a lot of space in my junk drawer. Be sure to reorganize your drawers before you put any items back in. There are some simple and affordable draw organizers on Amazon that makes finding things much easier.

Closets

This is my favorite area to clear out, so I make sure I do all my closets at least once a year. **Remember, the rule of thumb is if you have not used that item in the last year then most likely you're not going to use it or need it!** I'm always surprised how many people hold onto clothes they do not fit in anymore, because they're hoping that one day they will or they're saving it for a rainy day or special occasion. When you come across these items, try them on immediately to see if they still fit, make sure you PLUG IN to your Higher Source Energy, and then ask yourself, "Am I holding onto this outfit because of a good memory associated with it, or because it looks good on me NOW? Is this a current style that I'd want to wear tomorrow; does it itch or rub me wrong in some area; does this go with my current complexion and hair color?" As a hairstylist I learned that our hair and skin changes as we age (about every seven years), so if you have had items longer than that it may not suit you. That said, if you're wearing it at least once a month and you feel good in it then that is all that matters. When I first started this cleansing technique for my closet, I was amazed at how many items actually looked better on the hanger than on me. So be honest with yourself, and if you need a second opinion ask a family member or your team.

Third ACTION STEP: Release Immediately

- Donate it
- Sell it on eBay, consignment stores, Craigslist, or at a garage sale *and use the money to buy new stuff you love.*
- Trade with your family, friends or your team members!

Rearrange and redecorate with the items that are leftover, that are still LOVED. This is one of my favorite things to do because I actually feel like I went shopping and bought new stuff when all I did was move things to new and different areas of the house!

Lack Mentality Will KEEP YOU IN LACK

When you're re-creating your life, yourself, and the energy that surrounds you, it is true that "less is more!" Remember, the goal here is to surround yourself only with things you love and make you feel good! If you find that you are going into lack mentality (i.e. feeling afraid to let things go because you think you won't be able to replace it) CANCEL that thought and DELETE these words immediately by saying the following:

"I BELIEVE and TRUST in my Higher Power to supply me with whatever I need when I need it!"
Or, "I NOW RELEASE THESE ITEMS easily and effortlessly to allow my HIGHER POWER to replace them with what I TRULY NEED and WANT!"

During this time, it is critical to get positive energy flowing in and around you, especially in your house. This is *not* the time for you to block this energy with negative, limited thinking or concerns of lack. Remember, this is how you got stuck mentally, physically, or energetically in the first place. Releasing and letting go of unused items or things that are no longer energetically aligned with you is always the QUICKEST ACCELERANT to YOUR NEXT BEST STEP TOWARD YOUR MIRACLE!

Also, I have found when I donate items, IT ACTUALLY SEEMS TO BRING MORE MONEY TO ME, through other avenues, than when I sell it! Try this for yourself and see.

I NOW *Cancel*
and *Delete* all
negativity
from
MY HEALTHY
Life!

✂

I NOW *Easily* and

Effortlessly

release the *Old*

to

WELCOME THE

New!

✂

Chapter 8

Good Old-Fashion Diner

*I*magining you and a friend are at a well-respected diner. The chef is called GOD (Good Old-Fashion Diner) and is known for making anything you want to eat. The waitress comes to your table and says, "What would you like God to make you for dinner tonight?"

You reply, "I would love your best vegetarian burger."

Your friend replies, "I would like whatever your special is."

"No problem," the waitress says, "Enjoy your drinks and I'll be back with your food in a while."

Five minutes later…

You start to wonder, "Did I tell the waitress a vegetarian burger or did I just say hamburger? Because I'm a new vegetarian, and I'm not sure if I mentioned that. Maybe I should find her and ask, because if she brings a hamburger, I won't be able to eat it!"

You sit and wonder about this for ten more minutes…

You finally decide it's better to be safe than sorry and look around for the waitress but don't see her anywhere. You get out of your seat and walk around the restaurant looking for her, but she is nowhere to be found.

Fifteen minutes later…

You decide to go into the kitchen and confirm with God, the chef, exactly what you ordered for dinner. Just when you are about to push open the door to the kitchen you see your friend waving at you to come back and sit down. As you approach the table you can see your dinner has already been served, exactly the way you wanted! Your friend tells you your dinner has been here waiting for you for fifteen minutes, then excuses herself, saying she has an appointment and has to leave. As she gets up, she announces that it was the best dinner she'd ever had!

You finally sit down to enjoy your dinner and find that it is indeed the most delectable veggie burger you've ever seen. Unfortunately, your food is cold and you are now sitting alone.

You NOW realize...

You missed out on an enjoyable evening with your friend all because you didn't trust yourself, or the waitress, or even God the chef.

You NOW see...

The dinner with your friend represents YOUR LIFE and everything that is important to you.

The waitress represents your PRAYERS and your ability to RELEASE all your wants and needs to your Higher Power.

God the Chef represents your BELIEF and ABILITY TO BELIEVE TO RECEIVE, in every aspect in your life without trying to control it.

The magic of *Believe IT to Receive IT* relies on the power of your intention to walk every day towards the light in your life or any idea that makes you feel GOOD, HEALTHY, HAPPY, PROSPEROUS or LOVING, while at the same time not giving energy to and ignoring the darkness in your life—depression, illness, fear, lack, pain, hopelessness, perfectionism and any other idea that makes YOU FEEL BAD, unimportant, or not good enough.

By doing this you take back your power and you become the POWERFUL CREATOR YOU ARE MEANT TO BE IN YOUR LIFE!

"If you believe, you really see whatever you ask for in prayer."

Matthew 21:22

What If I Am Not Receiving My Miracle Yet?

If you have done all the ACTION STEPS in this book and you realize you have more areas to work on OR you're NOT as close as you want to be to Believing and Receiving your IT (Inner Transformation), please consider the following:

- You may have been too specific in trying to micromanage the "chef" in your life or your results (i.e. expecting your Higher Power, answers, or miracles to look or show up in your life a particular way).
- You may be sabotaging yourself by actually preparing for and confirming what you DO NOT want to be true in your life.
- Ask yourself if you are TRULY SOLD on this New Ideal Life Vision from Chapter 3. Or, "Did I create goals that are not really desirable to me because what I truly want seems too outrageous or unattainable?"

If so,

Take a DEEP BREATH and then blow the air out while mentally releasing all your worries, concerns and control. Then PLUG IN to your Higher Power and ask for guidance for Your

Next Best Step!

If you're so guided, read this book again to activate a deeper level of transformation or to transform a new area of your life. Please start over from the beginning and find yourself a new team so that you can empower one another during this MIRACULOUS TRANSFORMATIONAL PROCESS.

Then promise yourself you WILL BELIEVE with your whole heart and soul, so that you can RECEIVE YOUR MIRACLES THAT HAVE BEEN WAITING FOR YOU! And, that you will do your ACTION STEPS as if your IDEAL LIFE DEPENDS on it, because it does!

In Closing

If at any moment you are in doubt, and feel alone, please know that you are NOT ALONE, I created this book for you in the hopes that anyone who needed it would find it, and could see through my experiences that life isn't easy but it is possible to overcome your obstacles, make improvements and, yes, "call in" some MIRACLES along the way.

Remember, at one time *"from the depths of my soul I had a secret"*; at one time I lived in darkness and depression; at one time I needed and wanted a healthy, light, bright, positive community but I couldn't find one. This is why I created the *Believe IT to Receive IT* Facebook community so that you would have a safe place to go, where there is only positivity and love sent your way; a place with others who are BELIEVING IN MIRACLES TOO, BECAUSE THERE ARE NO OTHER OPTIONS!

It took me twenty years to understand this *"journey of my soul"* and to create this book, which has led me to you! Please know that from the deepest part of my heart, I BELIEVE in you and your ability to RECEIVE YOUR MIRACULOUS TRANS-FORMED LIFE!

I leave you with two final affirming mantras to help you reprogram your life as you CALL IN YOUR MIRACLES!

Sending love and blessings your way,

Bernadette Rodebaugh

HOW TO ACTIVATE YOUR LIGHT

When you want more light in your life, which is ALL THINGS that make you feel GOOD, think about those things OFTEN, and find ways to talk and walk towards those thoughts, hopes and dreams (or, at the very least, INTEND to).

This is especially important during the darkest moments of your life. REFUSE to let the darkness overcome you, because at that moment, with that decision, is when your INTERNAL LIGHT is ACTIVATED and acts as a beacon in that inner tunnel of darkness, calling in your hopes, dreams, answered prayers, and miracles so that they can find YOU.

"I AM A MIRACLE MAGNET IN EVERY AREA OF MY LIFE"

—Believe IT to Receive IT!

About the Author

Bernadette Rodebaugh is an author, coach and "The Miracle-ologist" with a mission to guide and remind you that you are the MIRACLE MAGNET in your own life. Through her personal experience Bernadette has learned that miracles are an inside job; however, one must first BELIEVE and SEE THEIR MIRACLE as they CALL IT INTO THEIR LIFE. She teaches the everyday TOOLS to do this in her professional, personal coaching, workshops and mastermind groups. Bernadette is also an intuitive and teaches you how to use you own internal guidance system to be guided to YOUR NEXT BEST STEP toward the miracle you are seeking. As her teachings are not tied to any specific religion, they can be utilized by anyone, regardless of their spirituality or belief system.

In her previous twenty-three-year-career as a hairstylist, Bernadette was amazed by how many people shared the most intimate details of their lives with her. She also observed their belief that only changing their appearance, their hair, or other superficial attributes that alone would change their lives, then they would attract the right relationship, great job, and so on. As a hairstylist, Bernadette helped them create the physical changes; as an intuitive she would often give divinely guided suggestions and tools that would help them uncover the, "NEXT BEST STEP" of the real issues they wanted to change in their life.

This profound way of guiding people to work on themselves from the inside out and create longer-lasting, healthier changes motivated Bernadette to retire as hairstylist and help people on a more profound level as their Miracle Coach.

Bernadette resides in Grand Junction, Colorado, with her husband, son and her rescued pit bull. As mentioned in the dedication, her other dog, Duke, died during the editing of this book. Bernadette still collects the heart-shaped rocks, now paints positive healing mantra words to them to remind others they are loved and not alone! She sells them at her events and donates all profits to various mental health organizations and animal rescues. Bernadette truly believes the unconditional love of an animal when paired with someone with mental or other health challenges creates a healing atmosphere where two lives are changed forever, and it's debatable who saves who! Learn more about Learn more about Bernadette at www.bernadetterodebaugh.com.

Continue the Miraculous Transformation

In 2021, Bernadette will begin releasing her follow-up books and oracle cards in the *Believe IT to Receive IT* series, each of which is geared toward helping you create miraculous outcomes in a specific area of your life, including:

- Health
- Wealth
- Life Purpose
- Love & Relationships

Bernadette also offers:

- Miracle coaching for individuals or groups
- Intuitive readings for 60 or 90 minutes
- Mastermind groups for *Believe It to Receive It* series
- Myers Briggs-Type Indicator Personality Assessments
- Archetype Assessments
- Your Soul Purpose Blueprint with Intuitive Reading

To find out more information, please visit:

TheMiracle-ologist.com

Miracles@BernadetteRodebaugh.com

Believe IT to Receive IT Facebook group

Download your FREE Miracle Tool kit

Here: www.believeittireceiveit.com

Acknowledgments

To Mom and Dad, thank you for believing in me when I did not believe in myself!

To my husband, Jarod, without whom this book would not be possible. Thank you for supporting me in every way possible with regard to My Ideal Life Vision, my business and this book. Thank you for showing me how to believe in myself and to always dream Big, Bold and Unapologetically. You are my hero and my earth angel. Thank you!

To my son Jaden, I know without a doubt, you and I chose one another for this lifetime! Your birth inspired me to ask more from myself and my Higher Power for every area of my life. Just having you as a part of my life has gotten me through many dark nights of my soul. Thank you!

To Aunt Bena and Aunt Condy, thank you for being my other moms and helping me through the darkest time in my life. Please know that doing my dishes, helping me with my laundry and all the other seemingly little things that over-whelmed me as a new mom with health issues made all the difference in the world to me! It helped me focus on my IDEAL LIFE so I could get better, and eventually write this book!

To Rita (aka my work mama!), you are the hardest-working woman I've ever met! Thank you for being my Earth Angel, helping me build a business and career during a recession! I do consider you one of the miracles I prayed for! Thank you for answering the call!

CPSIA information can be obtained
at www.ICGtesting.com
Printed in the USA
BVHW061054240820
587154BV00011B/846